READING THIS IS PROBABLY THE MOST FUN YOU CAN HAVE WITHOUT BEING ARRESTED.

The man who laid waste to the suburbs in his bestselling ANYBODY WHO OWNS HIS OWN HOME DESERVES IT now ranges further afield in his second bestselling book—a wickedly barbed, riotously funny attack on the sacred institutions, pompous professions, and furious frustrations of modern living that are fast closing in on us all. Nothing is spared—from weddings and doctors and telephones to sex and big business.

HELP! I'M A PRISONER IN A CHINESE BAKERY

ALAN KING

WITH JACK SHURMAN

AN AVON BOOK

Dedicated to my father, BERNARD, who for seventeen years never opened his mouth in the house and to my mother, MINNIE, who for seventeen years hasn't known that my father has not opened his mouth in the house.

AVON BOOKS
A division of
The Hearst Corporation
959 Eighth Avenue
New York, New York 10019

First Avon Printing October, 1965
Fifth printing, February, 1966

Printed in the U.S.A.

CONTENTS

FOREWORD

HALF THE FUN of taking the family out for dinner in a Chinese restaurant is the Ritual of the Fortune Cookie.

As soon as the waiter puts the plate with the four cookies in front of us, there's sort of a breathless anticipation as we each break open our own crisp little treasure and pull out the slip of paper inside. Even my nine-year-old son knows better, but I think that all of us harbor the secret belief that the future is going to be revealed.

Andy, the youngest, always goes first. *A thousand paper dragons have not the courage of one cowardly man.* Andy picked himself a loser.

Next comes Bobby. *You will find happiness in a new friendship.* Bobby is pleased.

Then Jeanette. *Take advantage of your exceptional talent and skills.* She puts that "see-didn't-I-tell-you?" smile on her lips.

Finally me. I'm always the topper, because I get a very grave expression and make a big ceremony of the reading. Bobby and Andy give each other a "here-we-go-again" look, because they know already that, no matter what it says on the paper, I'm going to come up with the same old line every time. *HELP! I'M A PRISONER IN A CHINESE BAKERY!*

It's really an ancient gag, but it still gets laughs. It's so completely incongruous that it's funny. And yet there's something there that's a little bit uncomfortable and something there that's rather sad that the kids wouldn't understand. It's too easy to identify ourselves with this guy and ridiculous dilemma, because we're all trapped in a Chinese bakery of a sort.

"We're all prisoners of the new society—or, rather,

what I prefer to call "the system and its institutions." As the system gets bigger, we all get a little smaller. Today we're all numbers on a punch card. Next year they're going to make us fractions. After that . . . ?

We're prisoners of the Bell Telephone System, General Motors, IBM, the American Medical Association, the airlines, J. Walter Thompson, Sigmund Freud, the Internal Revenue Service, the pollsters, the hucksters, the repairman, the discount store, our families, big business, big government, suburbia, the PTA, and sex.

This book is my own little fortune cookie. Like the man in the Chinese bakery, I get the feeling that there's no escape, but I've gotta try.

If I can laugh at "the system," I can always keep it in its proper perspective. Then there may be hope for all of us.

At this very minute, help may be on the way.

I doubt it.

But that's the way the fortune cookie crumbles.

HELP! I'M A PRISONER IN A CHINESE BAKERY

CHAPTER 1

MORNING
BECOMES ELECTRIC

I THINK A MAN deserves the Congressional Medal of Honor every time he wakes up in the morning. And, if he's married, they should throw in the Bronze Star with an Oak Leaf Cluster for each child under twenty-one.

Do you know what kind of guts it takes just to climb out of bed and face reality? I'll tell you something. I know men who would sleep their lives away if they had a choice. As long as they're sleeping, they haven't got a care in the world. Bliss and tranquillity all night long. The minute they open their eyes. Pow! NIGHTMARES!

Alan, leave me money . . . Daddy, Andy hit me on the head with a baseball bat . . . REAL-ESTATE TAXES TO RISE 112 PERCENT . . . Alan, the dog threw up in the living room . . . I'm sorry, Mr. King, but the car needs a whole new frammis . . . Daddy, the principal wants you to come to school today . . . If you've already paid this bill, please ignore the attached court order . . . Alan, my mother is coming to spend a month with us.

Who needs it? I don't even understand it. I've gone as far as to do research on how other people wake up in the morning. I've read great novels where the hero "arose as the buttercups were stirring their petals."

Or, "He greeted the rising sun."

"He awoke to the mockingbird's trill."

And how's this one? "The alarm clock gently nuzzled him from his reverie."

Do you know how I get nuzzled from my reverie? Lying in bed with my wife is like playing footsie with the Abominable Snowman. Her feet are covered with a permanent layer of frost. Seven o'clock in the morning she plants those feet in the middle of my back and starts to shove.

"Alan, get up."

"Get those feet out of my back."

"Alan, get up."

"I can't. I'm very sick. I'm staying in bed."

"Alan, get up."

"WHADAYA TRYING TO DO, FREEZE MY APPENDIX?"

"Cold feet, warm heart, Alan."

"One out of two. That ain't bad. WILL YOU STOP ALREADY WITH THIS ALAN-GET-UP ROUTINE!"

"Alan, get out of bed."

"I am out of bed."

"You haven't moved a muscle."

"GET THOSE FEET OUT OF MY BACK."

"Alan, get up."

"OKAY, I'M UP. I'M UP. I'M UP!"

How's that for a delightful way to start the day? Do you think she's waking me for my own good? She wants me to get to work on time? She doesn't want me to miss an appointment? Don't kid yourself. It's the only way she can get my pillow. Jeanette goes to bed with a hot-water bottle, three quilts, and the bedspread. Ten minutes later she's got my blankets and both sheets. And that's in the summer.

If the room temperature goes below 85 degrees, her breath begins to steam. In the winter she sleeps under the mattress. One end of the bedroom is filled with tropical plants. It's growing like a jungle. This may be great for Tarzan, but for a young Jewish boy, it's murder!

Now, under the best of circumstances, I do not rise and shine. In the first place, I've smoked about a pack of cigarettes and a dozen cigars the day before, and I don't exactly taste like a hint of mint. Whenever I go to the movies and watch Rock Hudson spring out of bed and kiss Doris Day before either of them have brushed their teeth, my stomach drops two feet.

Then, of course, the first thing I see when I open my eyes is this little bundle of fluff lying next to me with the covers pulled up to her eyebrows. The top of her head looks like it's been wired to go into orbit. Her hair is wrapped around some springlike contraptions which are really the shock absorbers from an old Hudson station wagon. If she's pointed in the right direction, her scalp will broadcast police calls from as far west as Minneapolis.

To make matters worse, I usually get up with a splitting, pulsating head. It's not a hangover. This is what they commonly refer to on television commercials as a "tension headache," and you usually get a tension headache from looking at television commercials about tension headaches. I get them because I don't go to bed until I watch the eleven-o'clock news, and that's usually the climax to a perfect day.

Last night I found out there was a hurricane in Florida, a riot in Georgia, Asian flu in New York, and the stock market had its worst day in a decade.

On the lighter side of the news there was a revolt in Rawalpindi that could touch off a third world war. To make matters worse, I don't know whether Rawalpindi is a fungus or a suburb of Chicago.

So this morning I got up again with a roaring tension headache. The whole world was poised at the abyss. Humanity stood at the crossroads of salvation or destruction. And I had a decision to make.

Should I take two Bufferin which would open those little trapdoors in my tummy? Should I take two Anacin and thrill to the exhilarating absorption of a combination of medical ingredients? Should I take two plain aspirin which tests by an independent laboratory have proven effective but not upsetting to my upper digestive tract?

There seemed to be only one solution. I took two of each. My headache went away immediately. I passed out for twenty-five minutes.

There I was, prone on the bathroom floor. The first

13

thing I heard as I regained consciousness was the plaintive voice of my wife—a sound that has about the same effect as chewing a tinfoil gum wrapper with a mouthful of gold fillings—saying, "Alan, get up. Alan, get up."

She was still in the bedroom. It was rather reassuring to know that she was kicking the stuffings out of the damned dog who had climbed under the covers at the same time I had climbed out.

I was a little sorry my headache was gone. All I had left was a postnasal drip, heartburn, and sore kidneys. I stood there with a coated tongue, eyeballs that looked like a road map of North America, and tried to decide whether I wanted to brush my teeth with a toothpaste that contained GL-73, hexochlorophine, stannous fluoride, Flabistan, irium, or chlorophyll.

I chose the toothpaste used by Group A which had developed 38.3 percent fewer cavities. You've seen the advertisements. This little girl comes running up to her mother shouting, "Look, Ma. No cavities!"

I use this toothpaste because I happen to like it. I use it every morning. I'd be a fool not to, because right on the tube it says that this toothpaste has been "tested and found effective in homes like yours." I consider that a pretty broad statement.

Did you ever wonder how they managed to find a home just like yours? Can you imagine looking under your bed and finding the Board of Directors of the American Dental Association? Have you ever had the soul-shattering experience of being the first one up in the morning and finding that your toothbrush is wet? Group A has been using it.

But that's not all. It also says on the tube that this toothpaste "has been shown to be an effective decay-preventive dentifrice when used in a conscientiously applied program of oral hygiene and regular professional care." Now there's a forthright endorsement of a product. It reads like a three-act play. That's the kind of statement that will go down in history with the other great slogans of our time—like "Win With Willkie" and "There's an Edsel in Your Future."

Most people go into the bathroom with the morning

paper. Not me. I read labels. If you buy the giant, economy-size products, you can stay in there most of the day.

In spite of the confusion involved, I consider brushing one's teeth a rather pleasant chore, and this morning I decided to go all the way. I'd use my new electric toothbrush which is guaranteed to vibrate 5,000 times a minute. I plugged it in and just stood there, watching the toothpaste flying all over the walls and ceiling. Man, that's a beautiful sight.

Next, I lathered my face with shaving cream, slipped a new blade into my razor and waited for the inevitable. The inevitable, in this instance, is what I commonly refer to as "the children's hour," and it begins at exactly the same time every morning with my nine-year-old son beating a steady tattoo of little fists on the bathroom door. My headache returned with a vengeance.

BANG, BANG, BANG. "Daddy, let me in."

"Andy, will you get away from there? I'm busy."

BANG, BANG, BANG. "Hurry up, Daddy. I've gotta. I've gotta."

"You can gotta in your own bathroom. Scram."

BANG, BANG, BANG. "Bobby is usin' our bathroom. Let me in quick."

I know when I'm licked. It took us seven years to toilet-train this kid, and I'm sorry we ever started. I really don't believe he's gotta do anything, but I know darn well that, if I don't let him in, he'll do it where he's standing, for spite. I opened the door.

Andy came flying in like a guided missile. I'd rather spend two hours in a broom closet with the Pittsburgh Symphony Orchestra than five minutes in the bathroom with my own son.

"DADDY, DADDY! GUESS WHAT I'M MAKING IN SCHOOL TODAY?" He's under the impression that the closer you get to a person the louder you have to talk. It's a habit he picked up from his mother.

"Let me guess. You're making earplugs for your father. STOP YELLING, WILL YOU? YOU'RE STANDING RIGHT NEXT TO ME!"

"Whatcha doing, Daddy?"

"I'm shaving," I answered, although I really wasn't,

15

because the lather had dried on my face and was starting to flake away. I washed it off and lathered up again.

He pretended he didn't hear. "Know what, Daddy? Lester Friedman has two new guppies wanna hear a joke what's green and black and brown and white will you buy me a new football I need a flashlight for Cub Scouts I broke Mr. Howell's window. QUICK, DADDY. LOOK OUTSIDE. THERE'S A BALD EAGLE IN THE CHERRY TREE!"

I jerked my head toward the window, but all I could see was the reflection of my own face and the rivulets of blood running down my neck.

I measured him for a backhand punch, but he got the message and disappeared in the direction of the kitchen.

Finally, I rinsed the blood from my face with an after-shave lotion extracted from the sexual glands of a bull elephant. Fighting the temptation to kiss my image in the mirror, I returned to the bedroom to finish dressing. This was going to be a little difficult, because I had mistaken my wife's hair spray for a can of spray deodorant. Now I couldn't get my arms down at my sides.

Jeanette's voice filtered up through two pillows. "Don't turn on the light."

"I beg your pardon."

"Don't turn on the light," she repeated.

"Why not? I've been looking at you for eighteen years. You can't scare me too much now."

"Alan, if you turn on the light, I'll wake up, and I won't be able to go back to sleep again."

My wife lives in darkness. She walks around all day with sunglasses; she goes to bed at night wearing two lightproof eye patches. We're the only house in the neighborhood that still has blackout curtains.

"I'll use a flashlight," I suggested.

"No lights!"

"How about a match?"

"That's not funny."

Funny? Who's trying to be funny? Did you ever get dressed by the glow of a phosphorescent watch dial? Well, here I am. Millions of people have seen me on television. I've had top billing at swanky nightclubs. I've

16

given command performances for royalty around the world.

Big deal, huh? And what does it all mean? While my wife, the Mattress Queen, sleeps, I'm on the floor trying to *feel* the difference between a brown shoe and a black shoe.

I got on the subway the other day and three men offered me a seat. I couldn't figure it out until I realized I was wearing a skirt and sweater.

Well, every man has his limits, and I'm no exception. This, I decided, was the showdown.

"JEANETTE!" I bellowed. "IT'S NINE O'CLOCK. I AM TURNING ON THE LIGHTS WHETHER YOU LIKE IT OR NOT. I AM GETTING DRESSED, AND YOU HAVE FIVE MINUTES TO GET OUT OF THAT BED AND MAKE ME BREAKFAST. I AM STILL YOUR HUSBAND. I AM STILL THE MASTER OF THIS HOUSE. DO YOU HEAR ME?"

"Alan," she moaned, "I don't feel too good."

I had just lost the shortest showdown on record.

I'm sure she didn't feel too good. She was covered by seven blankets. She was lying in bed and smothering.

"Please, Alan," she pleaded. "I'm so tired."

She was starting to get to me. "Okay, honey, go back to sleep and I'll fix my own breakfast."

"Thanks, Alan. And while you're at it," she added, "will you make a couple of tuna-fish sandwiches for the boys to take to school?"

"That won't be necessary," I said. "I'll come home early and fix them a hot lunch."

It took me seven years to talk my wife into getting up and making me breakfast. Then it took me ten years to convince her that I'd be happier if she stayed in bed. Her idea of breakfast is juice, hot cereal, and coffee, and, while it's both nourishing and filling, the lack of variety every day in the week can be a little gagging.

For cereal she uses something called "instant" oatmeal. First she brings a pot of water to a brisk boil and adds five tablespoons of oatmeal. When the mixture fails to thicken, she adds five more tablespoons of oatmeal. As this begins to solidify in the pot, she adds two more cups

17

of tap water. Then she adds more oatmeal and transfers the entire mess into the largest pot in the house. When this starts to boil over, we all start flushing the overflow down the toilet. Jeanette begins to cry, and I open a box of cornflakes.

As for orange juice, my kids think it comes from a cow. They wouldn't know an orange from an orangutan. As far as they're concerned, orange juice arrives every Monday, Wednesday, and Friday with the regular milk delivery, but what devastates me is that all of the pulp has been strained out of it. All that's left is pure juice and little pieces of wax that flake off the paper carton.

Sometimes I get no orange juice at all. Last week Jeanette discovered a breakfast drink called "A.M." It comes in a can. It looks like orange juice. It tastes like orange juice. But it isn't really orange juice. For dinner there is another drink called "P.M." It comes in a can. It looks like grape juice. It tastes like grape juice. But it isn't really grape juice.

I must be a square, because there is something here I don't quite understand. In this vast, fertile land of ours there must be someone who still grows fruit.

I have a great idea. I'm going to put out a new product called "B.M." It looks like prune juice. It tastes like prune juice. But . . . !

Don't get me wrong. "A.M." and "P.M." are not only nutritious, they're delicious, too. I've gone as far as to drink "P.M." in the A.M. Sometimes I drink it to get rid of the taste of Jeanette's coffee. One taste of Jeanette's coffee would convince you that her specialty is really "instant" oatmeal. It smells something like mocha Life Savers dissolved in swamp water.

When she opens a can, she transfers the coffee to a canister and uses the can for bacon drippings. One morning she made a mistake and percolated the bacon drippings. I wouldn't have known the difference, but the toast kept sliding down my throat before I had a chance to chew it.

This morning, however, Jeanette had made it clear that if I wanted breakfast I'd have to make it myself. Under the circumstances, I was looking forward to it.

The boys, who have permission to make their own breakfasts when their mother sleeps late, were already in the kitchen.

Andy was eating pretzel sticks and chocolate-ripple ice cream. Bobby had a piece of lemon meringue pie and a box of peanut brittle. I decided that I could forego the myriad pleasures of eating with my own children, and, by an amazing exhibition of self-control, I made it all the way back to the bedroom without getting violently sick.

"Good-by, dear," I whispered into a bulge of the blanket where I imagined her head might be.

"Umph!"

"Have a nice day."

"Umph!"

"I'm going to kill myself."

"Umph!"

"I'll see you at the potato harvest."

I could hear her grinding her teeth. "Alan, did you pick up your mess? The cleaning woman is coming today."

This is some cleaning woman. She keeps a spotless house. Before I leave in the morning I make sure that everything is spotless, and she keeps it that way until noon. I can always tell when she's been around, because the refrigerator is empty and her dirty lunch dishes are piled in the sink.

I picked up yesterday's socks, shirt, and underwear from the floor. I had no desire to see them there when I got home that night. Then I went to the closet and slipped on my raincoat. The sky was blue and cloudless, but I had a feeling that this was the kind of day where, if it rained nowhere else, it was going to rain on me. I resisted the temptation to chuck the whole thing and climb back into bed and sweet oblivion.

Taking a deep breath, I opened the door and stepped outside. Now I was alone. It was me and the world, and I muttered half out loud, "Come on, World. I'm ready for you."

Somewhere deep inside I seemed to hear another voice. It said, "Who are you kidding, Alan baby? Who are you kidding?"

I hopped into the car, turned the key in the ignition,

19

and pressed on the accelerator. The silence was oppressive. I tried again with the same results, only this time the key broke off in my hand.

Now some men might find this a little disturbing. I guess I was annoyed, but I really wasn't too surprised. It happens quite often—like every time Jeanette uses the car. What continues to amaze me, however, is that she never runs out of gas until she's parked the car in the garage.

Actually, I wasn't sure, at that point, whether the car was out of gas or the battery was dead. This morning I was twice blessed. The car was out of gas and the battery was dead, too.

I looked at my watch. It was 9:15.

I cradled my head in my arms and cried softly.

My God. The day had only begun.

CHAPTER 2

AFTER YOU SAY "I DO"
... YOU DON'T

HAS IT EVER occurred to you that the greatest loves of history and literature had one thing in common? The boy and the girl never got married.

Think it over. Paris and Helen of Troy, Tristan and Isolde, Cyrano and Roxanne, Antony and Cleopatra, Don José and Carmen, John and Christine. I could go on.

Not only don't they get married, they virtually never see each other. The lovers are always kept apart by family, society, wars, crusades, the black plague, or they're married to someone else. If you want to read about love and marriage, you've gotta go out and buy two separate books.

Romeo and Juliet, they got married. They spent one night together and the next day he committed suicide. Then she committed suicide. I'm trying to figure out what went on in that bedroom. That's a hell of a way to start a marriage. Can you imagine what this epic romance would have been like if they had to live together like normal people?

"Aren't you going to shave, Romeo?"

"It's Saturday; why should I shave?"

"Because my mother is coming over, that's why."

"You mother doesn't shave on Saturday either."

"And on your way out, take the garbage with you."

"Who's going out?"

"You are. My mother wants you to pick her up."

How's that for romance? No more of this "Wherefore art thou, Romeo?" jazz. She knows damn well wherefore he art. He's hiding in the garage trying to figure out why he ever got married in the first place.

I think that all these romantic classics do more harm than good, because the kids read them in school, and they grow up with a warped outlook on life. We should be teaching them that marriage has many advantages, too. I can't think of any offhand, but I'm not a teacher. Let 'em do their own research.

Look, I think I can speak from experience. I've been married for eighteen years. That's a fact. Jeanette and I just celebrated our eighteenth wedding anniversary. You know how every anniversary is associated with a material symbol—the fiftieth is golden, the seventh is copper, the tenth is tin. Well, the eighteenth is iron. If you can stay married to my wife for eighteen years, you've got to be made out of iron.

I don't ever remember being single. My wife and I were kids together. I've known her since she was seven years old. We both lived in tenements. We grew up in the same slum together. Of course, to look at my wife today you'd never dream that this was her background—unless you talk to her. Then, right away, you know where she came from.

I remember how much her father was against our marriage. He wanted her to marry a doctor, and, now that I look back on it, he was right. She should have married a doctor. It's the only way I could ever have gotten even with the medical profession. Furthermore, her father didn't want her to get married below her station. Jeanette's station was Fourteenth Street, and I had to get off at Eighth Street. That was six blocks below her station.

Obviously her parents weren't crazy about me. You'd think that marrying their daughter was a great big status symbol. It just so happened that my family had more money than her family, and we were on relief. So you can imagine what a big thrill they were.

The more I think about it the more I think that someone could have written a great novel about the two of us. We had all the elements. Her family opposed the marriage. They sent her on a boat trip around Manhattan Island. Maybe she'd forget about me. Maybe she'd meet another man. But all that happened, we were more in love than ever. We were going to get married, and there was nothing they could do about it.

The smartest thing we could have done was elope, but Jeanette wouldn't hear of that either. "We've got to do it right," she insisted. "Go ask my father for his blessing."

What an experience that was. Getting my father-in-law's blessing to marry his daughter was like getting the Governor of Alabama to give his blessing to a Freedom Bus.

"Your honor," I said, doing a little curtsy, "your daughter and I are in love and we want to get married."

Right away he started with the wailing. "My little baby; she's going to be married."

It was a very touching performance. "Don't cry, sir. Try to remember you're not losing a daughter; you're gaining a son," I said.

"THAT'S WHAT I'M CRYING ABOUT, YOU BUM!"

He had one more standard question. They've always gotta ask it. It's part of the ritual.

"Will you support my daughter in the manner to which she's accustomed?"

"Sure," I replied. "We're moving in with you."

Now Jeanette and I were officially engaged. That was the easy part, because when you get engaged there's a whole routine you've got to go through. The next night, for instance, I had to bring my parents over to Jeanette's house to meet her parents. That was Funsville, too. My mother brought along an album of my baby pictures. If you can imagine baby pictures being pornographic, you can imagine what these looked like. I don't know what my mother was trying to prove, but beyond a shadow of a doubt she proved it.

Jeanette's father broke out four bottles of bock beer that he had been saving for just such an occasion. Jeanette and I didn't say a word all night. We just sat there and listened to our parents lie to each other.

23

"Alan has always been such a wonderful son," my mother volunteered. "I couldn't have asked for a sweeter, more devoted, more considerate child."

I thought my father was going to throw up.

"I can't tell you how thrilled we are," my future mother-in-law said. "Jeanette has turned down so many proposals of marriage. Her father and I were afraid she was setting her sights too high."

"Boy, were we wrong," her father added.

"They're both so young," my mother said. "I hope that Alan decides to finish law school."

Five years ago I decided not to finish law school—about the same time I decided not to finish high school.

"I'm sure, Mr. King," Jeanette's mother said, "that you'll do everything you can to help the children along financially."

"I'd like to," my father replied, "but I'm afraid I just had a rather big loss in the market."

A truck hit his pushcart.

On the way home that night my mother passed her approval. "Nice girl," she said. "A little skinny, but nice." My mother's definition of a little skinny was any girl who could make her knees touch.

I jumped to Jeanette's defense. "A good wife doesn't necessarily have to be fat, Ma."

"When they're scrubbing floors and wringing the clothes, it don't hurt 'em to have a little meat on their bones."

I didn't say a word. My mother would never understand that, somewhere between the first and second generations, a fantastic metamorphosis had taken place.

Everything was set. Jeanette's mother decided to have a small, simple, impressive wedding limited only to the immediate world. She was having it catered by Barnum and Bailey.

And the excitement! You never saw such excitement. Renting the hall, preparing the menu, flowers, music, shopping for clothes. My wife and her mother found a place that was having a sale on wedding gowns. She bought two of them. I should have known what to expect already.

But that was just the beginning. Guest lists, invitations,

announcements in the papers, renting tuxedos, getting the photographer, buying the ring, getting a license.

This business of getting a license is pretty stupid. If you want to get a driver's license, you have to memorize a 102-page manual. You've got to take a test and an inspector goes with you. You have to park. Before that you've got to get a learner's permit. Why don't they give you a learner's permit before you get a marriage license?

The most important thing in anyone's life is marriage. You walk into the License Bureau. No test. No inspector. You give the clerk four dollars and he doesn't even look up. There could be two men standing there—as long as one is shorter than the other.

Now the first problem in making a wedding is trying to figure out who to invite, and, since the bride's family was paying for the wedding, they also controlled the guest list. They invited third cousins from her aunt's second marriage. They invited the guy that printed the invitations. But when it came to my guest list, my mother-in-law suddenly got very practical.

"You gotta keep it down," she advised me.

"Do you mind if I invite my mother and father to the ceremony? If it's too tough, I can have them stand on the roof and they can listen through the air shaft."

For the wedding, Jeanette's folks had rented the big hall in the basement of the local community center. Actually, it was only half a hall, because the room was partitioned off to accommodate a bar mitzvah celebration in the other half. We had the best part of the deal, because the basketball hoops were on our side of the partition.

Seating arrangements turned out to be a major problem. The guests were divided into eight armed camps. Aunt Fanny's family wasn't talking to Aunt Esther's family. Cousin Becky's family wasn't talking to Mildred Fingerman's family. The Frumkins once took a summer vacation with the Epsteins and fifteen years later they still weren't talking to each other. Uncle Newton was suing Uncle Monas for selling him a car with a cracked block. They both came with their lawyers. The Zuckermans were snub-

bing the Minskys because the Minskys' kid hit the Zuckermans' kid in the mouth and bent his braces.

My relatives and friends were sitting on the right side
of the room. Jeanette's relatives and friends were sitting
on the left side of the room. The aisle ran down the
middle of the room like the Yalu River.

The ceremony itself was really very impressive. My
mother-in-law decided that her niece Little Gertrude, was
going to be the guest soloist. Little Gertrude was fourteen
years old, a fat, homely kid with stringy hair. And to look
at her, you wouldn't believe she had the worst voice you
ever heard in your life. She sang "Because," and it should
have been "Why?"

According to the plan, this was the signal for me and
the best man to enter inconspicuously through a side door.
We'd wait then in front of the altar for the rest of the
procession and the final symbolic moment when I'd step
forward and take Jeanette from her father's hand.

The best man was Slob Gutterman, probably my oldest
and closest friend. I remember how I turned to him and
muttered something like, "This is it, pal. Let's go."

But Slob didn't move. He stood rooted to the spot.

"I think I'm going to faint." he informed me.

"You think *you're* going to faint? I'm the sacrificial
lamb at this orgy. How do you think I feel?"

"Alan," he said, "I've gotta go to the john."

"WILL YA FORGET IT, AND LET'S GET OUT
THERE ALREADY?"

"I can't help it. Wait right here. I'll be back in a
minute."

Slob disappeared like the proverbial bat out of hell. I
tried to signal the organist to stall for time, but I couldn't
even find her. She was completely hidden by twenty
potted palm trees so the guests would think the music
came from heaven. With the first strains of the wedding
march a hush fell over the audience. The procession
started.

First came my friends, the ushers, in their rented
tuxedos. As soon as they entered, the whole room smelled
like a mothball factory. They all wore top hats and carried
canes. They would have been more comfortable with a

26

cue stick in their hands. They looked like six delegates from the waiters' union.

Then came Jeanette's six friends, the bridesmaids. I never realized why I thought my wife was so pretty. It was because she had the ugliest friends you ever saw.

My mother and father were the next ones down the aisle, both of them proud as peacocks. My mother had a big frozen smile on her face. My father looked pained. He had forgotten to take the pins out of his shirt. I hoped they wouldn't be too disappointed when they found out I wasn't going to be there. I was still standing outside the hall waiting for my best man.

After my parents came Jeanette's bachelor uncle, Max, escorting my maiden aunt, Rachel. They looked like they were made for each other—Rachel with the broken slip strap hanging out the armhole and Max with the dried shaving cream under his ear and the piece of toilet paper stuck to his heel.

They were followed by Jeanette's parents. My mother-in-law was grinning bravely, but she couldn't control the tears that were streaming down her cheeks. My father-in-law was counting the house and mentally multiplying by $7.50 a head. When he had it figured out, he started to cry, too.

Jeanette's mother and father turned to await the grand entrance and the arrival of their daughter. A hush fell over the assemblage as the organ began the strains of "Here Comes the Bride." All eyes were now glued to the back of the room and, as the organist hit a crescendo, a pair of majestic-looking double doors swung open slowly, ethereally, and Slob Gutterman walked in. I think he was still looking for the john, because he was carrying his tuxedo jacket over his arm. As soon as he realized where he was, he turned around and fled in terror. I left my position outside the hall and went tearing after him.

On the way I passed Jeanette. "You go ahead," I told her. "I'll be there as soon as I can."

The organist was on her sixth chorus of "Here Comes the Bride" when my bride started down the aisle. She was a vision of loveliness in one of her two dresses. The audience went "ohhh" and "ahhh." They always do that at weddings. They sound like they have asthma. On both sides of the aisle you could hear the chorus of whispers: "Isn't she beautiful?" Of course she was beautiful. Did you ever see an ugly bride? Never, because they all wear veils.

Now everybody was accounted for except the groom and the best man. The organist had finally finished with "Here Comes the Bride" when she spotted me and Slob entering the hall. She didn't know what the hell to do. She got so shook that she started to play the only thing she knew how to play without the sheet music. It was probably the only wedding in history where the guests arose in the middle of the ceremony and sang "The Star-Spangled Banner."

Now Slob and I began the long walk to the altar, arm in arm, holding each other up. You should have seen me. Top hat, white tie, and tails. I looked like a Jewish penguin. Glancing around, I could see that at least half the people there were crying. Did you ever notice that the people who cry at weddings are the ones who are already married? It's the kind of thing that gives the groom enough confidence to destroy himself.

Of course, as you walk down the aisle, you've always got friends whispering words of encouragement.

"Hey, Alan, you can still back out."

And there's always the big mouth. "YOU'LL BE SORRY!"

Then the rabbi started: "Dearly beloved, we are gathered here to join this man and woman in holy wedlock." I was having a little trouble hearing what he was saying. Next door at the bar mitzvah celebration a thirty-piece Latin-American orchestra was playing the "Walter Winchell Rhumba." In the back of the room the caterer was starting to set up the tables for the wedding banquet. I thought he could have waited.

After a five-minute intermission, because the photographer couldn't get his flashbulbs to flash, the rabbi continued: "If anyone here can show cause why these two people should not be joined in matrimony, speak up, or forever hold your peace."

If I knew then what I know now, I could have talked for two hours.

All the time the rabbi was speaking, strange groups of people kept joining us at the altar. They were part of a guided tour being conducted by Mr. Spiegel, the rental agent for the hall, who was trying to book the room for a wedding the following week.

"For better or for worse," said the rabbi.

"We can fix the place up to look a lot nicer than this," said Mr. Spiegel.

"In sickness and in health," said the rabbi.

"That's a pretty lousy rabbi," said a man who was obviously not one of us because he was wearing Bermuda shorts.

"Do you mind if I get married?" I asked.

"Business is business," said Mr. Spiegel.

The rabbi then delivered a brief sermon on the responsibilities of marriage, the joys of children, the real meaning of the Ten Commandments, and a short history of the Old Testament. He wound up with a plea for tolerance in the world, a plug for his new book, and a condemnation of congregations that won't pay their rabbi a living wage.

"Jeanette," he asked, "do you take this man, Alan, to be your lawfully wedded husband?"

Jeanette said, "I do."

"And, Alan," he asked, "do you take this woman, Jeanette, to be your lawfully wedded wife?"

Jeanette said, "He does."

Then he handed me a little glass with a few drops of wine that I was supposed to sip. By this time what I really needed was a good blast of bourbon. Next, according to custom, the groom takes the wineglass, puts it on the floor, and steps on it. This is supposed to drive away the evil spirits. It didn't work. I looked up and my mother-in-law was still standing there.

"Alan and Jeanette," intoned the rabbi, "I now pronounce you man and wife."

Throughout the room you could hear a murmur of appreciation as I turned to kiss the bride. The rabbi extended his hand and said, "Mazel tov."

The best man said, "Congratulations."

My brother-in-law said, "When do we eat?"

Eat? You'd think that was the only reason for the wedding. You should have seen this spread. Jeanette's mother made all the arrangements, and we had a lovely buffet table. There were two swans carved out of ice. By the time we got to them they were melted down to pigeons. We had a heart carved out of chopped liver. It was no ordinary chopped-liver heart. This one was beating. Everybody was afraid to touch it.

There was chopped liver, chopped herring, gefüllte fish, hard-boiled eggs, stuffed derma, knishes, chicken soup with the fat congealing on the top so you could have skated on it, boiled beef, pot roast, and roast chicken. That was the first course. My mother bought matzo balls. They tasted like hockey pucks.

The *pièce de résistance* was karnatzela. You know what this is? Roumanian sausages. They're deadly. They were used by the OSS during the war when their agents were captured behind enemy lines. They had a little karnatzela kit. Rather than be tortured, you ate one of these things. It was faster than cyanide.

The booze was from my grandmother's basement. They used to call her Bubbie the Bootlegger. A couple shots of this bathtub hootch and your eyebrows fell off.

For music, my mother-in-law had hired Harry James and his orchestra. Only it really wasn't Harry James; it was Jeanette's cousin who had changed his name for business reasons. No one was too interested in hiring Herman Lifshitz and his Society Five. When the occasion demanded, he also booked himself as Stan Kenton, Lionel Hampton, Guy Lombardo, and Ina Ray Hutton.

About the best thing you could say for Herman's combo was that it drowned out the Brazilian Symphony on the other side of the wall. And talk about amazing coincidences—the guy who was playing for the bar mitzvah party was Herman's brother, Xavier Cugat.

Now the first dance, as you know, always belongs to the bride and groom. I'll never forget it. As I held Jeanette in my arms and waltzed across the floor, little stars twinkled in my eyes. The damned photographer

30

shot off a flashbulb three inches from my nose. After that I danced with Jeanette's mother and Jeanette danced with my father. Jeanette danced with her father and I danced with my mother. Jeanette danced with her uncle and I danced with my father-in-law. Then everybody began to dance.

It was like a three-ring circus. The women danced with the women. The men danced with the men. A drunken waiter was dancing with himself. The ushers were goosing the bridesmaids. Someone's nine-year-old kid who thought the Mogen David wine was Kool-Aid passed out on top of the wedding cake. My brother-in-law took over the microphone and was singing "I'll Be with You in Apple Blossom Time" while the band played "I Love You Truly."

In the middle of all this pandemonium the band broke into a *hora*, the traditional Jewish folk dance for all festive occasions. What's traditional about it is that the people who are dancing never have the slightest idea what they're doing. They all join hands and form a big circle. Then there's five minutes of free expression while they run back and forth yelling and bumping into each other. The banquet hall not only looked like a gymnasium, it was beginning to smell like one.

I didn't really care. I was happy just watching all my good friends having such a wonderful time. Moments like these, you can really appreciate your old pals.

Let me tell you all about my old pals. A bunch of jokers. My best man had already called the hotel and canceled my reservation for the night. One of my dearest buddies took Jeanette's father off in the corner and told him, *confidentially*, that I had received a medical discharge from the Army as a latent homosexual. Another old friend took Jeanette's mother off in a corner and told her, *confidentially*, that I had given a Trappist monk $10 to take my Wassermann test for me. And my own brother broke the news to Jeanette that I had a perforated heart. Any kind of physical exertion must be avoided at all costs.

I finally managed to catch up with Jeanette, myself, about one in the morning. "Honey," I cooed in her ear, "it's getting sort of late. Maybe we should leave."

31

"I'm having a wonderful time," she informed me, "but you look awfully tired. Why don't you go home and give me a call in the morning?"

"I'd like to, but I'm afraid I can't see you anymore. I just got married."

"Well, be careful of your perforated heart," she said with a knowing wink.

"How about one last dance, for old time's sake?"

"Why not?"

We danced with both arms around one another. Jeanette put her head on my shoulder and closed her eyes. Each time we twirled, I moved her a little closer to the door.

. . . past Aunt Bessie who was stuffing her purse with cold hors d'oeuvres.

. . . past Uncle Max who was stuffing his pockets with the stainless-steel silverware.

. . . past Aunt Sonia who was stuffing a floral centerpiece up the back of Uncle Herman's tuxedo.

. . . past a waiter who was fighting with my father-in-law. "AND I'M TELLING YA, THE TIPS ARE NOT INCLUDED WITH THE MEAL."

That was eighteen years ago, and that's the last time I danced with my wife. Boy, how time flies. In seven or eight more years my older son, Bobby, could get married and make me a grandfather. Knowing this kid, I hope he does it in that order.

In fact, just the other day I found Bobby poring over the pictures in the wedding album. He had a very puzzled expression on his face.

"Gee, Dad," he said, "if you and Mom were getting married, how come everybody is crying?"

"Bobby," I replied, motioning him to take a seat on the sofa next to me, "let me tell you a story.

"Once upon a time there were two families, the Montagues and the Capulets . . ."

CHAPTER 3

PUT YOUR HAND
ON MY TUMMY

THERE'S ONLY ONE THING in the world that men find more difficult to understand and harder to cope with than a woman. And that's a pregnant woman.

I don't care who the man is. He can be a bus driver, a fireman, a five-star general, or a captain of industry. The minute his wife says, "Honey, guess what?" he's had it.

For nine months he's a fixture around the house, an accessory to the fact to be tolerated as long as he doesn't get in the way. For nine months he can get lost and nobody will miss him. All he's got to do is drive the car back and forth to the obstetrician and make certain that he's available on the big day.

He can never know what it feels like to be pregnant. He can only guess what his wife goes through during delivery. All he knows is that his wife is going to be a mother, and there's nothing more sacred than the institution of motherhood.

Whatever she wants, she gets. You don't argue with a pregnant woman. Right away she points to her stomach and says, "I needed this?"

My wife used to turn sideways and give me the profile. "Alan King, just remember who did this to me."

I was so proud, I had to plead guilty.

A man's whole pattern of behavior during his wife's

pregnancy has nothing to do with reality. He's gotta walk around like a bungling, mumbling idiot or he's not playing the game. It's very important that he looks and acts stupid.

You see it all the time in movies and on television. The husband comes home after a hard day at the office and finds his wife knitting little booties. There's a coy smile on her face. She looks like a cross between Whistler's mother and Mona Lisa. At dinner she mentions that they should start looking for a larger house. In the middle of the night she wakes up with a craving for dill pickles and sour cream.

Now this guy is no fool. You don't have to hit him over the head.

"You mean . . .? Sweetheart, are you . . . are you . . .?"

"That's right," she whispers. "We have been blessed."

Mind you now, that's what it's like in the movies. But more than four million real babies are born in this country every year. Do you want to know what really happens?

"If you don't put that cigar away, I'm going to throw up."

"What's your big trouble?"

"I'm pregnant."

"The hell you are!"

"The hell I'm not!"

"Keeerist!"

I remember how my wife told me the first time. It's the kind of thing that a man never forgets. I came home from work and Jeanette was waiting for me at the door.

"Alan," she said, "the rabbit died."

"My God, Jeanette," I gasped, "that's terrible. How did it happen?"

I couldn't figure out why she was so indignant. "Alan King, just how do you think a rabbit dies?"

"Rabbit? I thought you said 'rabbi.'"

I tried to appear surprised and happy. Surprised, I wasn't. Happy? I was genuinely overjoyed.

"Jeanette, I assume that you're telling me you are pregnant, and I think it's just wonderful."

She put her head on my shoulder and started to cry. "Alan, I'm going to be a mother, and you're going to be a father."

34

"Both at the same time. How lucky can you get?"

As the story emerged, Jeanette had been to the doctor on Wednesday. This was Friday, and the announcement of the premature demise of the rabbit had come earlier in the afternoon. My wife, the doctor had indicated, was at least two weeks' pregnant—probably closer to three.

"Alan," Jeanette said as we sat down to dinner, "we mustn't let anyone know."

"I didn't think it was something you could hide for long," I observed.

"I didn't mean that. It's just that nine months is such a long time. It would be nice if we didn't have to make others wait that long with us."

"That's very thoughtful of you."

"We won't say anything until I'm three or four months pregnant, okay?"

"Okay."

"It will be our secret."

"Our secret."

"Promise me, Alan. You won't say a word."

"Not a word."

The phone rang, and I answered it. It was Jeanette's mother.

Jeanette put a finger to her lips and winked slyly. I slyly winked back as I handed the phone to her.

"HELLO, MOTHER," she screamed, "I'M PREG-NANT!"

In the next two hours Jeanette shared our little secret with her mother, my mother, Aunt Rose, Aunt Estelle, Aunt Clara, Aunts Etta, Eva, Yetta, Zetta, and Fanny.

Anita, Loretta, Phyllis, Roz, Margie, Lila, Betty, Peggy, Kiki, Mimi, Carol, Nancy, Ellen, Arleen, and Ruthie, Mona, Joyce, Millie, Zoey, Jo, Barbie and Joan.

At exactly 9:21 P.M. two critical wires in the telephone melted, and Jeanette gave up for the evening. The next morning Jeanette's pregnancy remained pretty much our secret. There was a drill-press operator who worked the night shift at a paper-bag factory in Chico, California. He still didn't know.

Jeanette, in the meantime, was telling everybody that her due date was in December, so they wouldn't get impatient if the baby arrived late. If you counted it off on your fingers, she was either going to be pregnant for eleven months or she wouldn't conceive for another two.

Jeanette's mother and father came over to the house to add their best wishes. Her father was sort of quiet. He just looked at me like I was the Mad Rapist of Hamburg. He had no idea I was sleeping with his little girl.

My mother-in-law threw her arms around my wife and sobbed, "My baby is going to be a mother. You've got to take it easy. Don't do any work. Be a lady for once. Him," she added, pointed at me, "he should have all the labor pains."

I think she meant it. I was just trying to figure out how she was going to arrange it.

My own mother took the news to be a challenge. She circled Jeanette three times and announced, "It's going to be a girl."

"Ma," I chided, "Jeanette is only three weeks' pregnant. You can't tell a thing."

"Well, let me ask you a question, Mr. Bigshot," she snapped. "Can't I always tell? Have I ever been wrong?"

Had she ever been wrong? She had never been right.

"Look," she said, slapping Jeanette on the rear. "When they're big in the rump, it always means it's going to be a girl."

That's the way my wife always looks. I was happy I kept my mouth shut.

My mother was chock-full with wisdom. "And don't forget," she reminded Jeanette, "you wear a piece of garlic around your neck so it should be a big, healthy baby."

If my wife had worn a piece of garlic around her neck three weeks earlier, she wouldn't have been pregnant now.

At the end of the fourth week I drove Jeanette to the doctor for the first time since she had learned of her delicate condition. The obstetrician's office looked like the auction pen at the Kansas City Stock Yards. I haven't seen so many different shapes since my folks bought me an erector set.

They were all slouched down in leather armchairs scattered around the reception area. I was the only man in the room, and they looked at me as if I was the one who was responsible for their condition. They would have had a lynching party, but none of them could get up.

I steered Jeanette to two seats in a far corner, and she sat down with a big sigh. Did you ever hear a pregnant woman sigh? It sounds like the last scene in *The Hound of the Baskervilles.*

Dr. Satzman emerged from his office, walked straight over to Jeanette and me, and extended his hand.

"I recognized you right away, Mr. King. I always like to meet the prospective fathers, so I can tell them all the things they should know about."

Dr. Satzman then proceeded to tell me all the things a prospective father should know about.

"Now you mustn't worry about a thing. My fee is $350. You can pay it all now, or before the baby is born, or you can even pay a little bit down on every visit."

"Do you give Green Stamps?" I asked.

Dr. Satzman stepped back and appraised my wife. "You're looking great," he said, pinching her backside. He wasn't getting fresh. He pinched all the women. The way most of them looked, it was the nicest thing that happened to them since their last visit.

"Come back in four weeks, and we'll weigh you," he said over his shoulder as he disappeared into his office.

I looked at Jeanette. "That was your examination?"

"Alan," she explained, "I was here just last week."

That I knew. I just thought that $350 was a little high for getting weighed. I remember when it used to cost a penny, and you got your fortune told at the same time.

On the way home we stopped off at a drugstore and picked up a bottle of calcium pills, a bottle of liver pills, a bottle of iron pills, a bottle of appetite-depressing pills, and a bottle of multivitamin pills. The pill bill ran to $47, and to this day we still have the full bottles stored away in the back of the linen closet.

"They make me nauseous," Jeanette informed me.

Evidently the pills were the only thing that made her nauseous. She had given up smoking, but it had nothing to do with morning sickness. She wanted to have both hands free for shoving food into her mouth. I've been to catered weddings where they served less food than my wife consumed in one evening watching the "Late Show."

She dropped her purse one day, and half a roast chicken fell out. She tried chewing gum and went through fifteen packages a day. That's a lot of gum. She was swallowing it.

Obstetricians, of course, are dogmatic when it comes to overweight. If a patient is getting too heavy too fast they really let her have it. They get tough, they warn, they threaten, and they scare the blazes out of her.

The women take it all very seriously, too. For twenty-nine days—malted milks, double hot-fudge sundaes, mayonnaise sandwiches with Russian dressing. The day they visit the doctor—nothing! They starve themselves so he doesn't know they've been overeating. They'll take the stays out of their corsets if they think it will save them half an ounce. Just before they leave home they stick their fingers down their throats.

Going into her fourth month, Jeanette decided it was time to start wearing maternity clothes. It wasn't what you would call an arbitrary decision. She couldn't get her garters within five inches of her stockings. Even her Playtex Living Girdle had died.

Now it wasn't too long ago that all pregnant women wore sort of a standard uniform called a Mother Hubbard. It looked like an army blanket with armholes. Every woman owned two of these, which was more than enough because she never went anywhere. You couldn't get her to leave the house.

Not anymore. Jeanette went shopping for maternity clothes like most women go shopping for a trousseau. She came back with eleven dresses, two formal gowns, a maternity brunch coat, maternity toreador pants, and three pairs of maternity slacks. In the sixth month the slacks are reversible. It doesn't make any difference if they wear them with the fly in the front or the back.

These maternity clothes are ingenious inventions. They usually consist of a skirt with a blouse that's worn outside the skirt to cover up a secret trapdoor. The trapdoor expands with a drawstring, and that's the key to the whole

38

thing. Every month they pull the rip cord, and another parachute opens up.

But I still haven't mentioned the real winner. This you've got to see yourself. It's a maternity bathing suit —affectionately referred to as the "Moby Dick." If she swims in the ocean, they sew an American flag on it so the Navy patrol boats won't open fire by mistake.

Up to this point Jeanette's pregnancy was rather emotionally uncomplicated. Except for the monthly visits to the obstetrician, very little had happened to change the course of our married lives. Then came midnight of the third day of the fifth month.

Jeanette began to shake me. "Alan, wake up."

"WHAT'S THE MATTER? WHAT'S THE MATTER?"

"Something's moving," she exclaimed.

"It's the cat burglar. Pretend you're asleep. When he comes in the door I'll hit him over the head with the . . ."

"Not downstairs, dope. Inside. I feel life, Alan. I feel life."

"That's great," I said, closing my eyes. "You should live to be a hundred."

She started with the shaking again. "Alan, put your hand right here."

"Yeah?"

"What do you feel?"

"Your belly button."

"That's not what I mean."

"I don't feel anything."

"It stopped now."

"Good night, Jeanette. I've got a big day tomorrow."

My wife, of course, had felt the first movements of the baby. To a woman, this must be both a thrilling and awesome sensation. She felt them again at 2 o'clock, 2:45, 4 o'clock and 5:30. I still hadn't had a drop of sleep.

"There it goes again, Alan."

"Jeanette, please. You're going to be pregnant four more months. I can't stay awake that long."

It was like talking to the sphinx. "There, there. Quick, put your hand on top of mine."

"Okay. Last time."

"Feel it move?"

"I sure did. Oh, boy. That's amazing. I distinctly felt the baby move. Very exciting. Good night, dear."

"Alan King! You did not feel the baby move. It's way over on the other side now."

"He's hiding. Maybe he wants to go to sleep, too. Will you leave him alone before he gets punchy?"

The first signs of activity on the part of the baby are always a signal for frantic action on all fronts. Birth is only four or five months away. That may seem like a lot of time, but there's so much to do, so many important things to decide.

Decisions. As soon as we got into bed Jeanette would reel off a list of decisions which had to be made that night. Whom should we invite to the bar mitzvah? Should he play high-school football? Where would he go to college? What if he got some girl into trouble?

"Jeanette," I'd implore, "for all you know it can be a girl."

"You're right. We're going to worry about that tomorrow night," she'd reply.

Surprisingly enough, one of the problems that we had no trouble with was a name for the child. We agreed on that from the very beginning. If it was a boy, it would be Robert. A girl would be Elizabeth. We agreed, but you should have heard everybody else.

"Robert? What kind of name is that for a boy?"

What kind of name? It's a name name. I don't know. Robert sounds awfully good to me. I remember when they used to call kids John, George, Samuel, William, Earl. When was the last time you heard of a baby being named Earl?

Today they've got to be different. You get crazy names like Agamemnon. That's different. But it's never Agamemnon Smith. It's always something like Agamemnon Fuchtwanger or Lilli Belle Shmoot. April Rabinowitz. Melody Klotz. If they give the kid a decent name, they've got to get cute with the spelling—Wilyam, Stefann, Mari Loo. Wilyam grows up, and he goes out to apply for a job.

"What's your name, son?"

"I'm not really sure, sir."

40

This kid's got some bright future.

Having the name all settled gave Jeanette time to come up with other ideas. I was becoming very wary of her ideas.

"Alan, we ought to turn the den into a bedroom."

"What's the matter with the room we've got for the baby now?"

"I was thinking that you and I could move into the den and give the baby our room."

"Do you really think he'll need a stall shower?"

"No, I just feel he should have more space."

Space? You buy a crib, and the baby lies in it. Maybe he waves his arms and kicks his legs. What kind of space?

Jeanette had her reasons. "Well, I'd sort of like one of those Louis XIV cribs with a canopy."

"What's with a canopy?" I asked. "Do you think the kid is going to tinkle on the ceiling?"

"We'll do the whole room in French Provincial," she informed me.

"I thought it would be nice if the baby was a United States citizen," I volunteered.

Jeanette's eighth month was distinguished only by the frequency of trips to Dr. Satzman. These had increased to one a week. The ninth month was distinguished only by the frequency of telephone calls from my mother-in-law. These had increased to one every half hour.

"Hello, Alan? What's new?"

"Do you mean since I talked to you five minutes ago or since the beginning of the year?"

"I just called to tell you that it looks like rain."

"I'm sorry to hear that."

"Is Jeanette there, Alan?"

"No, she isn't."

"WHERE IS SHE?"

"Relax, Mother. She's in the beauty parlor."

"ALAN, TELL ME THE TRUTH. DON'T LIE TO ME. I'M STILL JEANETTE'S MOTHER, YOU KNOW. SHE'S IN THE HOSPITAL, ISN'T SHE? SHE HAD THE BABY, DIDN'T SHE? WHY DIDN'T YOU CALL ME?"

I couldn't blame my mother-in-law for thinking I was

41

holding out on her. Every time she called, my wife was in the beauty parlor. The baby was due any minute now, and I was positive Jeanette was going to deliver under a dryer. God forbid they should wheel her into the delivery room with a limp head of hair.

On top of this she was out every day shopping for new clothes to bring to the hospital. She didn't take that many nightgowns on her honeymoon. I don't know whom these women try to impress, because, in the hospital, all they've got is one another. They act like they're going away on a five-day vacation.

The day the baby is born, they slip into silk negligees, fancy robes, and fluffy new bedroom slippers. They get dressed up like beautiful dolls. Then they lie there for the next four days and moan about their stitches.

Well, like I said, the doctor had told Jeanette that her due date was November 2. Somewhere along the line somebody forgot to tell the baby, because he sure didn't know. On November 12, 13, and 14 I took my wife for long rides over gravel roads in the country. The only things I shook loose were an axle and three of my own teeth. Jeanette never felt better.

Of course, this couldn't go on forever and, obviously, it didn't.

On the sixteenth of the month I came home from the city and found Jeanette sitting on the sofa with her coat over her arm and the suitcase at her feet. This was it!

"Alan," she said, chewing at her lower lip, "I'm getting pains."

I tried my best to appear calm and in complete control of the situation.

"How often?"

"Every forty-five minutes."

Actually, I had been rehearsing this moment for a long time. The first thing I did was call Dr. Satzman. Then I alerted the hospital, called my mother-in-law, my mother, and the nurse we had hired to look after the baby when Jeanette came home. I called Jeanette's sister and asked her to contact the diaper service, the milk company, and the drugstore, and to order the layette as soon as she got word whether it was a boy baby or a girl baby.

Everything that I could think of had been done. By 10 P.M. Jeanette had made considerable progress.

Three days later I packed her into the car and off we flew.

That was some ride. One in the morning. The hospital was twelve miles from our home and I made it in twelve minutes flat. "Jeanette," I said, "you wait here in the car. I'll go for help."

"Hurry, Alan, hurry," she whispered, and I went tearing into the hospital and up to the front desk in the lobby.

The receptionist looked at me like she never saw a man in his pajamas before.

"Lady," I panted, "my wife is having a baby."

"What room is she in, sir?"

"She's out in the car."

"Well, what can I do for you?"

"Kiss me. I haven't had any loving for months."

"You want your wife admitted?"

"Yeah, yeah. Now you've got the idea."

"Have you been to the admitting office?"

"LADY, I HAVEN'T BEEN TO THE TOILET FOR THREE DAYS. ALL I WANT IS THAT SOMEONE SHOULD GO OUT AND GET MY WIFE SO SHE CAN HAVE A BABY."

"I'm sorry, sir. But you must go to Admitting on the sixth floor. Please use the elevator over there."

I ran back to the door and peered out into the street. Jeanette was looking out the car window for some sign of me.

"I'LL BE WITH YOU IN A MINUTE," I shouted. "DON'T GO AWAY."

Then I turned back into the lobby and ran to the elevator.

Did you ever wait for an elevator in a hospital? The cable could break, and it would take ten minutes to drop from the second to the first floor. It takes five minutes for the door to open all the way. When you finally get into the elevator, the smell of ether could knock you out.

The admitting officer pointed to the chair next to his desk. "Have a seat, Mr. King."

"My wife is having a baby," I mumbled.

43

"Congratulations," he said, pumping my hand. "I'm going to have to ask you a few questions."

"Look. Go get my wife. I'll fill out your questionnaire. How's that?"

"Do you have Blue Cross, Blue Shield, major medical or private medical insurance?"

"I've got a new plan. It's called 'Money.' WHO DO YOU HAVE TO KNOW AROUND HERE TO HAVE A BABY?"

"Believe me, Mr. King, there's nothing to worry about. Whom should we contact in case of an emergency?"

"Your family doctor," I replied.

"*My* family doctor?"

"That's right. Because if you don't take care of my wife in one minute, I'm going to tear you apart."

"You don't seem to understand, Mr. King. Your wife has been in the labor room for a half hour already."

"She has?"

"Of course. We wouldn't let her sit out in the car. She's going to have a baby."

"I forgot."

At 10:30 A.M., Monday, November 19, 1952, Robert King was born. The attending physician was Dr. L. D. Rittenberg, night intern on duty at the hospital, who filled in for Dr. L. R. Satzman when he ran out of gas on the Long Island Expressway.

CHAPTER 4

PLANNED CHILDHOOD

OVER THE YEARS I've read hundreds of reports—psychological and social studies—on the behavior of children. I'm interested, of course, because I have two sons of my own. I also have a morbid curiosity about the psychological and social behavior of some of the nuts who have nothing better to do than write these reports. I don't think they know what they're talking about.

On one hand, they tell us that today's youth is insecure and immature. For proof they point to the alarming number of young men who can't adjust to military training. Take them away from their mothers, and right away, eighteen years old, they start with the bed-wetting.

On the other hand, we're informed that youth today is aggressive and hostile. The experts point to the growing incidence of juvenile delinquency. You can't walk through a city park today without a police escort.

I think these psychologists should make up their minds. Are the kids insecure and immature, or are they hostile and aggressive? Why don't we take the juvenile delinquents and draft them into the Army? Let them have a constructive outlet for their hostilities.

Then we could take all the mama's boys, give them butterfly nets, and everybody could enjoy the parks again.

The reason for all the research on children is to find out why so many kids are going wrong. They spend millions of dollars studying the youngsters, and they always end up pinning the rap on the mothers and fathers. Just yesterday I saw a headline in the paper that fascinated me.

"ANTISOCIAL KIDS BLAMED ON PARENTS"

The article reported on a study by a prominent psychiatrist who proved, dramatically, that 77 percent of all problem children come from families where there is no adult supervision. It's an interesting theory, but before this guy jumps to any conclusions I'd like him to come out and see what adult supervision is doing to the youngsters in my neighborhood.

You know, all the problems do not come from slum areas and broken homes. The middle-class suburban communities could use some social workers, too. If my two sons could have ridden with Pancho Villa, Pershing wouldn't have had a chance.

But no one can figure out why a child who has all the advantages in life should ever get into serious trouble. When he does, the reaction is always the same. The shocked father throws up his hands and cries:

"I don't understand. We did everything."

It just so happens that he's right. The typical kid in my neighborhood goes to the best schools, gets a good education, comes from a happy home with all the opportunities, grows up socially acceptable, and he's equipped to do absolutely everything except earn a living.

This is the kid who goes to work in his father's business. From the time he's ten years old, he's been brainwashed. Every night the old man comes home bemoaning his destiny.

"I've worked hard all my life. I built up a business. Am I going to live forever? Who did I build it for? A stranger? No! I built it for you."

But first comes college. No one can figure out why the kid bothered to finish high school, but for sixteen years he goes to college. Finally, he graduates with a Ph.D. in business administration and goes to work for his father. So what does he do? Papa makes him a shipping clerk in the stockroom.

"I want that he should learn humility like I learned humility."

And all the old man does now is complain about his son.

"He doesn't take an interest."

One day the son does take an interest. "You know, Dad, I think if we cut velvet and changed our production system . . ."

The old man clutches at his heart. "HE'S GOING TO TELL *ME*? MY COLLEGE GRADUATE IS GOING TO TELL *ME* HOW TO RUN *MY* BUSINESS?"

I think we should realize that having parents plan out every step of their children's lives is not always a blessing. The big thing used to be planned parenthood; now it's planned childhood. We start with them when they're infants. Every hour on the hour Mother sings a little lullaby.

> Rockabye baby.
>   Go to sleep, honey.
> You'll be a doctor,
>   And make lots of money.

A baby lies in his crib sucking his toe, and it's the last thing he ever does without supervision. From there on in he leads a timetable life.

It's six hours in school and an hour for homework. Then they've got after-school schools and schools after the after-school schools. There's an hour of religious school and two hours of Sunday school. On top of this there's dancing school, music school, elocution school, and singing school. The current fad is singing lessons— for babies. One little girl in my community hit a high note and swallowed her pacifier.

Friday night it's the Boy Scouts, Tuesday night is 4-H. Wednesday, P.A.L. Twice a week YMCA and YMHA. These are all wonderful organizations, but since the kid left the womb he hasn't had five minutes to himself.

If a child shows a little sign that he's upset or nervous —right away to the psychologist. How did we ever grow up without psychologists? Even when there's no problem, they've got an answer.

"The boy is suffering from repressed sexual desires for his mother. That will be fifty dollars please."

Now I ask you, between the kid and the psychologist, which one is sick? You can save your money. Our children are nervous and upset because we won't leave them alone.

What's really happening is that we're raising a race of little Mr. Machines. Eleven o'clock they've gotta go here. Twelve o'clock they've gotta go there. I walked out of the house one day and saw my younger son with his thumb in his mouth, standing in the middle of the lawn like a statue.

"What's the matter with you?"

"I got an hour off. Nobody told me what to do."

It isn't bad enough that we've got to plan everything for our children, we've also got to participate in all their activities. My wife has no time for the house, and I've got no time for my own business. We've got to run with the kids.

Every other day I've got to go to school. Father and Son Day, Son and Father Day, Parents' Day, Teacher's Day, Open School Week, P.T.A. meetings. I spend more time in school now than I did when I was a kid.

To make my life complete, my wife keeps telling me, "You've got to be a pal to your sons." Why? Who cooked up this bit that you've got to be a pal to your sons? My father had seven boys. He didn't want his kids to be pals. He said he had enough friends.

What children want is some free time to play by themselves. If there's anything a child knows instinctively, it's how to play, but we've got to teach him that, too. When I was young, a gang of the guys would run into the schoolyard and choose up sides for a game of baseball. No one told us what to do. We just felt like playing ball. But that's all been changed.

Now they've got something new—Little League. Now the kids gotta play when their parents want them to play. They take happy-go-lucky youngsters and put them in the same emotionally charged atmosphere as professionals.

48

Farm teams, minor leagues, major leagues, world series, ulcers.

My entire life is wrapped up in the Little League. Even my house has been redecorated. It's a new style called Early Yankee Stadium. All over the place gloves, balls, bats. The imported French pillows are now bases, and my kids are running all around the house with their spikes. I've got to take off my shoes when I come into the house, but they run around in spikes.

I come home at night and these screwballs are hitting fungoes in the living room.

"THERE'S NO BALL PLAYING IN THE HOUSE."

But they don't listen. Who listens? I gave one of them a whack once that I'll never forget. Did you ever try to hit a kid with a catcher's mask on?

And my wife lets them get away with it. In fact, she encourages it, because Jeanette is the manager of the team. They picked her 'cause she looks like Casey Stengel.

All of a sudden the women are crazy about baseball. It seems that Little League has become a status symbol. Now it's "my son, the shortstop." And even if the kid doesn't want to play, that doesn't make any difference. He's gotta be on the team.

I remember how my mother never liked me to play baseball. She used to tell me, "Practice the violin. You'll hurt your golden fingers."

Today a kid says, "Ma, I wanna practice my violin."

She says, "SHUT UP AND PITCH."

The Little League season doesn't start until about the middle of April, but the fever sets in around March. That's when they have the first meeting to brief the parents. Every year I swear that the first meeting is going to be my last one.

They always hold these meetings in the unheated gymnasium of the local grade school. You sit like an idiot for two hours in those little kiddie chairs while they pass around a sheet of paper to sign so they know that you were there. They not only treat the children like adults, they treat the adults like children.

Then three flabby fathers wearing blue T-shirts with "OFFICIAL" on the chest introduce each other. They

49

take turns describing how the other two have given so un-selfishly of themselves.

"Remember, folks, your Little League officials have volunteered their precious time to help *your* children."

You know the definition of "volunteered." Nobody asked them.

Then there's a discussion of schedules and rules of play.

"All games will be played on Thursdays and Saturdays at public school 12. All games will begin promptly at 3:15 P.M. The children must be wearing regulation baseball shoes, or they won't be allowed to play."

They always open up the floor for questions. These are the questions:

"What days are the games played on?"

"What times do the games start?"

"Is it okay if they wear street shoes?"

The last subject on the agenda is equipment. Invariably, one mother stands up and asks, "What's a jockstrap?" Her husband gives her a crack with the elbow in the ribs. They pass around another sheet of paper to catch anyone who snuck out. Everyone goes home.

Actually, the subject of equipment should not be taken lightly. Do you have any idea what baseball gear costs today? A new glove costs $15—for leatherette—that's a Japanese word meaning "plastic." For $10 more you can get Mickey Mantle's autograph on it. Mickey Mantle paid only $9.50 for his own glove.

When I was a kid, I had a glove that was handed down from brother to brother. By the time I got it there wasn't enough padding in it to catch a ping-pong ball. Today, if the glove touches the ground, that's the end.

"IT'S DIRTY. I WANT A NEW GLOVE."

Did you ever see how kids break in new gloves today? When we were boys, we used to take axle grease off a wagon wheel and rub it in. My sons take two pounds of polyunsaturated, low-cholesterol corn oil and shmear it all over.

"How do you like it, Dad?"

"Great. Put a little salt on it. I'll eat it."

Most of the time you're lucky if they ever get the glove on their hand. They start out with all new equipment.

New bats, new balls. The next day they've lost everything. Do you think they care?

"Dad, on your way home from the office will you pick me up a new bat?"

"What happened to the bat I bought you yesterday?"

"I can't find it."

"WHADDAYA MEAN YOU CAN'T FIND IT? LOOK WHERE YOU LEFT IT. THAT'S WHERE YOU'LL FIND IT."

"I left it in the basket on my bike."

"So go get your bike."

"I don't remember where I left it."

These kids are always testing you to see how much they can get away with. I finally got smart. I told my son Bobby that the only way he'd get a new bat would be if he went out and earned the money himself. Sure enough, the next day he came over to me with $7.00. I was really very proud.

"That's my businessman," I said, throwing an arm around his shoulder. "How'd you get the money?"

"I sold your blue suit."

"OH, IF YOU EVER TAKE OFF THAT MASK, YOU'RE GOING TO GET IT!"

Actually, the cost of registering your child for Little League is quite modest. They have other ways of raising money. The mothers blackmail the local merchants into buying uniforms. My younger son plays for a team called the Great Neck Rappaports. On the back of the jersey is "Cleaning, Dyeing, and Alterations."

And they also raise money with raffles. Last year I bought $11,000 worth of raffles. Every five minutes a kid is at the door.

"Mr. King, sir. Would you like to buy some raffles?"

"I'm sorry, young man, but I just bought some."

"COMMUNIST!"

I really shouldn't complain, because I'm twice as fortunate as most of the fathers. I have two baseball players in my family. How's that for a blessing? One is in the major leagues and the other one started out in the minors. They practice on different days, play at different schools, and the parents meet on different nights. Fortunately, I happen to be a different kind of father. I don't go to anything. God forbid you should do for one kid and not for the other.

Mrs. Dean thought she had a Dizzy and a Daffy. You should see these nutty sons of mine. Bobby has been in the Little League for three years. My nine-year-old Andy just got into the Little League. Last year he didn't make the team because he couldn't answer the first question: Are you a righty or a lefty? We finally painted an R on one hand and an L on the other. Now he's really confused.

"Daddy," he keeps asking, "if I'm a righty, why do I wear the glove on my left hand?"

"What are you asking me for? When I was a kid, I played polo."

(I never played polo.)

Now while we're on the subject of organized play I've got to tell you about the first Little League game of the season. I think it's typical.

The game started at 3:15 Saturday afternoon. It was only a six-inning game, but I think it's still going on. When I left, the score was 84 to 23—in the first inning. One kid was pitching a no-hitter, but he walked a few.

What's cute as the dickens is that all the children do their best to copy the professional baseball players. They stand and they scratch themselves. In this league, when they send a kid to the showers, he really needs it. Once they're issued a uniform, they don't take it off. Between games they wear it like underwear.

They also chew tobacco, or at least they make believe they're chewing tobacco. It's really bubble gum, but with some of these kids you can't be too sure.

Now you've got to try to picture this. The Great Neck Rappaports were playing the Glen Cove Take-out Pizzerias and the Rappaports were up first. The lead-off batter was an eight-year-old kid about three feet tall and all of sixty pounds. Perfect coordination, good eyes, and a great swing. He only had one trouble. He couldn't lift the bat.

His mother was off on the sidelines yelling, "YOU GOTTA CHOKE UP ON THE BAT!" So he choked up. He had more bat sticking out on the bottom than there was on the top. The first pitch he swung, missed the ball, and rapped himself right in the belly.

The second pitch came down the middle and he really laced into it. The ball went dribbling past the pitcher, through the shortstop's legs, and out into center field. The center fielder raced in, picked it up, and fired it over the first baseman's head and into the street. The ball was retrieved by the catcher who threw it back into left field. The left fielder never saw it, because he was on his hands and knees looking for four-leaf clovers.

Fortunately, the right fielder was also covering left field by mistake. He promptly relayed to the third baseman who was posing for a picture for his father and stopped the ball with the back of his head. The second baseman threw the ball underhand to the pitcher who rolled it on the ground to the first baseman.

It wasn't even close. The batter was out by five steps.

The second batter up was the neighborhood rich kid. He wouldn't go from first to third unless his mother drove him in the station wagon.

My son Andy was the next batter, and he's no Ty Cobb either. Every time he swung he threw the bat. He cleared the whole schoolyard in five seconds. The coach kept telling him, "Andy, you've got to hold on to the bat tight." Finally he caught on. He started to run around the bases with the bat in his hand. Everybody was afraid to tag him out. He had a weapon.

The score was 18 to 0 before the other team lifted its pitcher, and it really wasn't his fault. The catcher kept waving his hand in the air and the pitcher thought he was calling for a slow ball. All the catcher was trying to do was signal that he had to go to the bathroom.

That's the way the whole game went. No one ever caught the ball, because they all tried to catch with one hand. They had to. With the other hand they were holding up their pants.

One kid was chasing fly balls in the outfield and his mother was running after him with a glass of chocolate milk. Another kid hit a home run, but his mother made him stop at second base because he was getting overheated.

Some of these children enter Little League, and they've never had a bat in their hands. They honestly don't have the slightest idea what the game is all about. It's a thrilling experience to watch them as the season progresses. They gain confidence and poise, and you'd be surprised how fast they catch on.

I never gave Andy much hope, but after three games he improved so much that they moved him up to the majors. You can imagine how thrilled he was to be playing on the same team with his brother. Regrettably, this all led to one of the most unforgettable experiences of my life.

The final game of the season I was called upon at the last minute to umpire. D day was more laughs for me. They used to have a regular umpire. He would have been thirty-five next month, but one of the mothers ambushed him with a hatpin.

This was really togetherness. Bobby was pitching, Andy was catching, I was umpiring behind the plate, and there was my wife, behind me, changing my decisions. Even here she wouldn't let me have the last word.

To make matters worse, every decision I would make, Jeanette would holler, "KILL THE UMPIRE!" What does she care? I'm heavily insured. I even called my own kid out on strikes. I had to sleep in the garage for four nights.

Now I can take this from my wife, because I'm used to it; but you should have heard some of the comments from the spectators. Even this didn't bother me. Everybody knows that sticks and stones can break your bones but names will never hurt you. As soon as the crowd sensed that I couldn't be intimidated by threats, I got treated with a new respect. They began to throw sticks and stones.

As the game wore on, you could feel the tension growing. Behind the bleachers a group of the more emotional fans were boiling a cauldron of tar. At a crucial point in the game I called one of the kids safe on a close play at home. I thought there was going to be a riot. Fortunately, someone had the good sense to whip out a Jew's harp and twang "The Star-Spangled Banner." It probably saved my life.

This Little League is a very serious business. As soon as the game was over, you never heard such screaming and hollering. For hours they screamed and hollered. These were the parents carrying on. The kids had gone right home. They couldn't have cared less.

Finally all of the spectators marched down to the Village Hall and burned me in effigy. To this day I'm still getting poison-pen letters. And don't forget, these games are all for fun.

I think we adults have to look at this thing honestly, because we're losing our perspective. You parents of Little Leaguers, you've got to accept the fact that not all kids can grow up to be Bob Fellers and Joe DiMaggios. The aim of Little League is to teach sportsmanship and fair play. Most communities try to run it that way, and, when they do, it's a great experience for everyone.

I'm afraid that this may come as a shock to some people, but Little League is organized for the children, not the parents.

So do yourself a favor. Your wanna play baseball? Start your own league, and leave the kids alone.

CHAPTER 5

ATHLETICS
ANONYMOUS

THERE'S A NEW status symbol out in the suburbs. Muscles.

For years suburbanites considered it chic to be flabby. That spare tire around the middle was a sign of affluence. It just meant that, whenever there was manual labor to be done, you could afford to have someone do it for you. It was "in" to be indolent.

But no more. A strong and vigorous nation needs strong and vigorous citizens. The Federal Government has called upon all of us to throw off our fat. Schools across the nation have joined in a crash program to develop young bodies and to make our children the strongest and healthiest kids in the world.

The President has appointed the head of a new Department for Physical Fitness. "The country," he said, "is getting soft." Well, I don't want to appear disrespectful, but who needs a hard Jayne Mansfield? The country should be in such good shape.

My wife knows all about physical fitness, because she was in great condition under Herbert Hoover. But let's be practical about this. Women don't have to be strong anymore. Women live in a push-button world. When a woman wants to get something done, she takes one finger and—RUMPH—she pushes it right into her husband, and he does everything.

Jeanette is always making with the finger. RUMPH—

"Aha! What's that roll around your middle, Alan King?"

"THAT'S MY MONEY BELT. YOU AIN'T GETTING YOUR HANDS ON THIS, SWEETHEART."

Do you know who stays in great shape? My father. He takes long walks in the fresh air. Every time he has a fight with my mother, he takes a long walk. In 51 years he's walked 83,000 miles.

A few weeks back both my sons came home from school with pamphlets marked "For Parents." Inside, in bold black print, was the question: "CAN YOUR CHILD DO THESE THREE SIMPLE EXERCISES?" Below this were pictures of some kid doing twenty-five push-ups, fifty sit-ups, and chinning himself ten times.

Look, I'm as patriotic as the next man, but why is everybody suddenly so concerned with the physical condition of the kids in America? What's the big deal about muscles? The next time you walk into your boss's office throw yourself on the floor and do fifty push-ups—see if you get a big, fat raise. The odds are ten to one they'll ship you off to the "funny farm."

So what are we preparing our children for? Are we planning to *wrestle* the Communists?

Today's child is a product of modern technology. He grows a foot taller than his father because he's pumped chock-full of vitamins from the day he's born. He gets shots to avoid 90 percent of the illnesses that afflicted his parents. He eats six balanced meals a day, sleeps fourteen hours, and spends three more on his back watching television.

Both my sons can do twenty-five push-ups without straining, but they haven't got enough energy to pick their clothes up off the floor. They can do sit-ups all day without breathing hard, but they haven't the strength to walk to school.

In fact, out where I live they don't learn to walk until they're nineteen. Any kid worth his salt drives to school in his own car, and when I say "car," I don't mean a family castoff or secondhand jalopy. The youngster with last year's model parks it three blocks from school and slinks the rest of the way in shame.

Do you know that one of the biggest problems in school

construction is where to put the parking lot? That's right. It's a major consideration. Our high school had to stagger the classes to break up the traffic jams. They have eight cops on safety patrol whose only job is to help the teachers across the street. All my friends think I'm very fortunate because I bought one car for both my children and talked them into sharing it. Unfortunately, neither of them will be old enough to drive for another six years. It just sits there in the garage, and we trade it in every September.

Since we live right across the street from the school, this poses no burden. The school bus picks up the boys and brings them home.

Does this mean, then, that our children are soft and flabby? Not necessarily. Getting in and out of those racy new foreign cars takes a lot of exertion. So just to make certain that Junior doesn't fall prostrate between lunch and recess, classes are arranged for a minimum of strain. They don't have to climb stairs anymore. They've got escalators. This is great for the leg muscles. Did you ever watch two thousand kids going from the first floor to the second floor on a "down" escalator?

Our school has a special bus. At the end of the day it takes the children from the escalator back to the parking lot. I ask you, who's to blame if children today are less than ambitious? America needs strong bodies and my kids are majoring in Rest Period.

Remember your own grade-school days and how you used to look forward to recess? Baseball, kickball, foot races, tag. What do you think they do now? I'll tell you what they do. They flip baseball cards. Now there's a real body-building exercise. My own son is champion flipper of the third grade. He's got so many muscles in his wrists that the pediatrician can't find his pulse.

This, of course, I can't blame on the schools. Monday through Friday it's their job to exercise young minds. This leaves Saturdays and Sundays for developing sturdy bodies, and, if you live in the suburbs like I do, it's weekends when you can really appreciate your healthy and vigorous children. When there's grass to be cut or windows cleaned, I can depend on my two strapping youngsters to stand there and watch me do it.

Every night I walk into the house and the first thing I hear from my wife is, "Alan, you've got to talk to the boys. I can't get them to do a thing."

So what happens? Saturday I hint that it would be nice if one of them took out the garbage. Right away I've got Jeanette to deal with.

"Oh, leave them alone, Alan. They're only young once."

That's just great. It does wonderful things for my prestige. Immediately she's the big hero and Daddy's a fink. Of course they're only young once. I'd just like to live long enough to be old once.

While I'm working years off my life expectancy on Saturdays, what do you think those kids are doing? Well, from 6 A.M. to 8 A.M. they're flipping baseball cards. From 8 A.M. to 9 A.M. they're watching the movie *Abbot and Costello Meet Frankenstein and the Wolf Man* on television. When I was their age my parents wouldn't permit me to watch horror movies. My own kids see a double feature before breakfast.

From 10 A.M. to noon more television. This time it's a program where the boys and girls of elementary-school age play "Pin the Tail on the Donkey" for $80,000 worth of prizes. Is it any wonder they don't listen to their parents? They're all independently wealthy.

Saturday afternoons are devoted to physical activity. They stand on the corner and look up and down the street for the Good Humor man. Saturday night they read comic books and torture the dog until he gets just mad enough to bite the baby-sitter.

If you think my children are lazy, come over sometime and meet my wife. There's a human dynamo. She won't walk two blocks to the drugstore for a pack of cigarettes. She won't even take the car. She calls up and has them delivered.

"For Pete's sake, if you don't want to walk, take the car. It's only two blocks."

"Now, Alan, you're being perfectly ridiculous. This is a free service the drugstore gives, and there's no reason in the world we shouldn't take advantage of it."

My wife has an idea that all these services come compliments of the management. I've been around long enough to know that anytime someone offers me a "free service" I want to settle for half.

"Whaddaya mean 'free'? I have to tip the guy fifty cents every time he comes over here with a thirty-cent pack of cigarettes."

"I'm a very good wife to you, and if it costs fifty cents to make me happy, you're a lucky man. It costs more than fifty cents to take the car out of the garage."

"You ought to try driving without the emergency brake on."

Three years ago I bought my wife a station wagon so it would be easier for her to load packages into the car when she went shopping. Two hundred cubic feet of cargo space. That's twenty-five dollars a square foot so she can haul around a golf bag, a bowling ball, and a gym suit. She's got to have all the equipment, because you don't know what's going to be fashionable next week. She takes up a sport and the first day she buys everything, all of the outfits, and then she gets tired of it. My house looks like a sporting-goods store.

With the government stressing physical fitness the way it has, the current craze for the ladies is the exercise club. They go there for workouts, massages, and hot-fudge sundaes in the snack bar. My wife goes with her girl friend Millie Berman. You have to see these girls. They run around in black leotards—they look like a Sherman tank in mourning.

Mind you now they call these things "exercise clubs," but the women don't do a thing. They just stand there. The machines do everything. They've got machines that run up and down you. They've got machines that shake you, bake you, spank you, and yank you. Three times a week Jeanette lies down on a table for a massage, and somebody slaps her around for five dollars a session. If she'd only give me half a chance—POW! WHAM! For nothing.

Well, women have taken over everything else, so, sooner or later, they had to take over all the sports, too. They're in the gyms and the pool and on the golf courses, all the places a man used to go to get away from women.

I love women at the golf courses. Did you ever have to

wait fifteen minutes in the middle of a sun-baked fairway because the woman in the foursome ahead of you lost her golf bag?

They take the game so seriously. They're out on the practice tee from sunup to sundown, and it's not cheap. I leave for work every morning, and my wife has a new battle cry. "LEAVE ME MONEY FOR THE CADDY AND THE PRO!" From him my wife takes lessons all day —$10 a half hour. Suddenly I've got a new dependent— a fresh-air gigolo.

After all the lessons and all the practice and all the money you'd think she'd play like a professional, or at least like she knew what she was doing. She swings—it would break your heart. She's got four distinct motions— backswing, downswing, follow through, and tug the girdle. Jeanette once teed off and hit a man 300 yards up the fairway. It wasn't her golf ball; she missed that. It was her driver. She let go of it when she swung.

Only one thing is more dangerous than a club in your wife's hand, and that's a bowling ball. There's something you shouldn't miss—my wife with the bowling. She walks around all day with her hand up in the air like she was taking the Girl Scout oath. She's resting her fingers.

I come home from a tough day at work and I want a little attention, a little love and affection. The first thing I hear is, "Hurry up and eat. I have a bowling tournament."

"I KNOW YOU DIDN'T HAVE A COOKING TOURNAMENT!"

Every neighborhood must have a bowling alley now. In my town they tore down a high school to put up a bowling alley.

"How are you doing with your bowling, sweetie?"

"I'm up to 187."

That's not her score; that's her weight. Bowling is an excuse for eating pizza pies.

Twice a week my wife plays golf. Wednesday nights, bowling. She spends so much time trying to improve her health that I'm losing mine. On top of this she makes two trips to the beauty parlor, once with her own head and once with a scalp she bought in a department store for

61

$200. She still manages to get in a round of tennis, the beach club, a floating canasta game, and classes in yoga.

My wife prepares her schedule with the same care they give to a rocket launching at Cape Kennedy. Since I work hard all week long, she not only plans her own activities, she plans mine, too.

I look forward to the weekends like I look forward to a sinus attack. There isn't enough grief Monday through Friday. Saturdays and Sundays I've got to worry about the storm windows, the garage, the basement, the flower beds, the car, and the plumbing. On top of this I'm expected to barbecue all the meals, including breakfast, and be a father to my children. Then I go to my in-laws' house and start all over.

Physically, I'm in great shape. It's my frame of mind that's sick.

What does my wife do on weekends? I don't know. She acts like she's just won "Strike It Rich." By 7:30 A.M. she's out of the house with her golf clubs, her bowling ball, and my wallet, and I don't see her again until the kids are in bed.

All I hear during the week is, "I'm bored. Why don't you talk to me? Why can't we do things together?"

She's right. We should do things together. Saturday morning I tell her. "Okay. You paint the ceiling, and I'll work on the walls. Then you pull the crabgrass, and I'll spread the fertilizer."

This goes over very big, of course, and she has a standard answer.

"What kind of man are you?"

I don't know. How many kinds of men are there? I didn't know I had a choice. If I'm anything, I'm the kind of man who thinks that even physical fitness can be carried too far, and, believe it or not, I finally got Jeanette to agree with me. No more golf and bowling, because it takes her away from the family. Now she's got something new. She's on a togetherness kick. Home exercises.

All day long she's stretched out—with the box of bonbons—wired to one of those electronic spot-reducing machines. Did you ever see one of those contraptions? She gets into bed with the wet pad around the middle and the wet pad on the thighs and the wet pad under the chin. Then she plugs herself in. Jeanette King, 128 pounds, 5,000 volts D.C.

Every night now I've got to go to sleep with this. I don't even get a jury trial.

"Gimme a kiss, dear."

ZZZZZTTTT!

"ONE MORE JOLT, WARDEN, HE'S STILL TWITCHING."

Let me tell all the women something. If you're really serious and you want a good exercise to keep in shape, I've got just the one for you. It involves bending, stretching, moving, pulling. It's called "housework." You ought to try it.

My wife just happens to be a great little housekeeper. There can be junk all over the house when she gets up in the morning. Ten minutes later everything is neat and clean. I used to wonder where she put everything, then I found out. Come over to my house sometime and look in my bureau drawers. Everything goes into the drawers. When she's finished dusting, the dustcloth goes into a drawer. Two weeks ago I wore it to work.

This sets some example for the children. If they're going to be the next leaders of this country, it's up to their parents to show them the way.

That's why I think we all ought to get together and back the President's physical-fitness plan. However, if it should just so happen that you're not really sports minded, there is another alternative. It's a club called "Athletics Anonymous."

If you get up in the morning with an uncontrollable urge to play tennis or handball or golf, you call up a member of the club. He comes over with a bottle of booze, and you finish the bottle while he talks you out of it.

CHAPTER 6

I'LL HAVE
20 CENTS' WORTH
OF ELIJAH MANNA

DID YOU KNOW that the number-one health problem in the
United States is obesity? That's a fact. We're all too fat.

You ask your insurance agent, and he'll tell you that
there's a definite relationship between weight and life expectancy. Personally, I'm not in love with the insurance companies, but, when they issue their Health Ad-
visories, I listen. They pool all their information and feed
it into a giant computer. When it comes out, you've got
one of those charts that shows exactly what you're supposed to weigh.

For example, if you are a woman, 5 feet, 6 inches tall
without shoes, 30 years old, dressed normally, you should
weigh between 115 and 135 pounds depending on
whether you're small, medium, or large and your mother's
middle name is Wolfgang. There's a definitive piece of
information. Small, medium, or large *what*? They never
tell you. That's a 20-pound spread. That's the difference
between my wife and Anita Ekberg.

The skinnier you are, the longer you're going to live,
and, according to them, I should weigh 83 pounds. Fortunately, I don't need their charts. I married a girl who
is always there to reinforce my conscience whenever my
willpower starts to wane. Her specialty is tact.

"Alan, you're starting to look like a fat pig."

She plays on my ego with all the subtlety and delicate finesse of a Jascha Heifetz playing on the violin with a pneumatic drill. According to Jeanette, only my side of the family is fat. On her side, they're all big boned. Her brother has a physique like the General Federation of Women's Clubs. He's got the biggest bones you ever saw, and they're all covered with big blubber.

Whenever my wife starts needling me about my weight, I get very defensive, and, of course, that's a mistake.

"So help me, Jeanette, I haven't gained a pound."

"Would you like to bet? Go step on the scale, and we'll see."

"WHO ARE YOU GOING TO BELIEVE, ME OR THE SCALE?"

I'll tell you something. The scale is a god in our house. And did you ever watch these women weigh themselves? They cheat. They bounce up and down on the scale until the springs get stretched out of shape. Then they start with the jumping and the jiggling until they get the weight they want. They play it like a pinball machine. What this country needs is a scale that lights up with a big "TILT!"

They have it down to a science. They can get different readings by putting the scale in different positions on the bathroom floor. Wanna lose five pounds, fast? That's seven tiles over and three tiles down. When they go to someone else's house, that's a different story, because they don't know the combination. Before they go into the bathroom, the first question they ask is, "How much is your scale off?" The answer depends on whether the hostess is overweight or underweight, because they all lie through their teeth.

Men can't fool around that way. They put on weight, and they start getting little potbellies. With the women, they can jam it and cram it into a girdle. Where the hell it goes after that, I don't know, but it has something to do with atomic fission. Jeanette has a girl friend, Rebecca Woolf, who's walking around right now with a critical pile. Any day there's gonna be a chain reaction. KA-BOOM! The end of the world.

Becky looks like a bag of heavy water, but she's the

one who runs around telling everyone else how *they* should go on a diet.

"You should eat nothing but cottage cheese for every meal . . .

"All you've gotta do is fry everything in unsaturated corn oil . . .

"You should go see this doctor. He's got green pills for the thighs, pink pills for the stomach, blue pills for the rump, white pills . . ."

Every week, Becky reads another magazine article, so every week Jeanette goes on a new diet. This would be fine with me except that everything Jeanette eats, I have to eat, too. First, it was the 900-calorie liquid diet. It's like wet chalk, and it's supposed to take the place of three square meals a day. My wife was on a diet, and I was going to bed with hunger cramps.

Between each meal, you can have a special, low-calorie cookie that's made up largely of cellulose. Cellulose is really indigestible, but it's supposed to fill up your stomach and depress your appetite. After dinner, you take out your home movies. You eat them.

And if you're still hungry, there's a no-calorie soft drink, no-calorie canned fruit, no-calorie pudding. After all these years, I've finally figured it out. Calories are what nature puts into food to make it taste good.

I wasn't feeling so hot, but Jeanette had no problems. She'd watch TV every night, and, at three o'clock in the morning she'd have a corned beef sandwich and a piece of cake. She figures if it's dark and nobody's watching, you don't gain weight.

Well, I don't believe in those idiotic fad diets. When I want to lose weight, I've got a formula all my own that never fails. I call it "Alan King's Three-Day Plan for a Slimmer, Trimmer You," and, although I don't recommend it as a substitute for a visit to your doctor, here's how it works.

First Day: I eat no breakfast and no lunch. This is a matter of practical necessity. All other reducing plans tell you to eat things like three small lettuce leaves with an eighth of a teaspoon of vinegar, three and a half ounces of lean hamburger, well done, a one-inch wedge of cantaloupe. This is fine if you own a chain of restaurants, but if you've got to eat at any of those glorious New York lunch counters, forget it.

"I'd like three and a half ounces of lean hamburger, well done, please."

"Which way do you want it to lean, Buster? To the right or to the left?"

For dinner on the first day, I come home and there's baked lasagna, veal parmigiana with a side of spaghetti, garlic bread, French fried potatoes and banana cream pie.

"WHAT ARE YOU DOING? I'M ON A DIET!"

My wife has a standard answer: "Don't eat it."

"WHAT'S THE MATTER? DO YOU HATE ME? ARE YOU TRYING TO TORTURE ME? WHAT AM I SUPPOSED TO EAT?"

"For goodness' sake, Alan, I'm not on a diet. The children aren't on a diet. Do you want us to get sick?"

Get sick? If they eat that meal, they'll rupture themselves.

Second Day: Again, no breakfast and no lunch. Dinner the second night at my mother's. With her, if you can finish the chicken soup without falling on the floor in a stupor, she's failed. Her standard fare is nine courses starting with cold borscht with a boiled potato, potato pancakes with apple sauce, blintzes with sour cream, and progressing to chicken with bread stuffing, fried kasha, candied yams, and bread pudding.

"What is this, a conspiracy? Ma, I told you I was on a diet."

"Tonight, you got a vacation. When you come here, you eat. Tomorrow, you can diet on your own time."

Third Day: I can't get out of bed. The doctor sends over an ambulance with a stomach pump.

Now you've got to admit that this whole diet routine has overtones of the ridiculous, because instead of eating sensibly, we stuff ourselves one day and starve ourselves the next. Whole new industries have sprung up just so we can have our cake and eat it, too. Today, these diet preparations are a big business, but even they don't hold a candle to the biggest gimmick of them all—health and miracle foods. I'm told that these so-called health foods take in about a half-billion dollars a year, and I can believe it, because, now, my wife is on a health-food kick like the rest of them.

Jeanette's hero is Robert Cummings, the movie star, and, according to her, Robert Cummings claims to be a product of health foods.

"See how good he looks—how young?"

He's like a Dorian Gray. I'd love to see the painting that he's got hanging in his attic.

Now she's got me crazy with health foods and roughage. You know what roughage is supposed to do for you. For a month I was afraid to leave the house. For years, I didn't know what people did with crabgrass. Now I know. They chop it up, and it's a health salad.

Do you want to hear about the thrilling dinner I had last night? I had a cup of alfalfa with honey. You couldn't get a horse to eat alfalfa with honey, but the health bugs, they eat everything with honey, because it's the only way they can get the junk to slide down.

I also had a beautiful plate of cracked wheat with a side order of seaweed, and, for dessert, I cheated. I licked an envelope.

It so happens that I just read an interesting article in the newspaper about this very subject. The Food and Drug Administration conducted a big study on health foods with a Harvard professor heading up the research. They reported that there's really no such thing as "health" food, because all food is healthy. There's some nutrition in everything we eat.

In other words, if you like sassafras juice, drink sassafras juice, but there's nothing wrong with orange juice, either, if you don't mind being a square. My grandfather used to get up every morning and for breakfast he'd have pickled herring, raw onion, and a shot of whiskey. He lived to ninety-three. He had the worst breath you ever smelled, but he was healthy.

How do you explain it? The government tells us smoking is bad, so we smoke more than ever before. The government spends a fortune, hires some of the greatest minds in the country, to tell us that there's no such thing a... health food, but we still shove this glop down our throats like it was the essence of life.

I've browsed through a lot of the health-food stores, and I made a list. I wrote things down, because I wanted to be accurate. Now, let's discuss some of the products these witch doctors tell us we should put into our stomachs. The facts. These things are authentic.

First, there's blackstrap molasses. It comes in jars, but it looks like it belongs in your crankcase. I looked it up in the encyclopedia. I don't fool around.

> BLACKSTRAP MOLASSES—The sticky, dark substance left in the bottom of the pot after they refine sugar. It's used to feed animals, as a road filler [you thought they used tar], and as a fertilizer.

Lots of luck!

Actually, the whole bit is one big contradiction. To get blackstrap molasses, you've got to refine sugar. But these health-food kooks insist that the only kind of sugar you should eat is *unrefined* sugar. This is very interesting. Under chemical analysis, the only ingredient that refined sugar doesn't have that unrefined sugar does have is DIRT.

To strengthen their argument, they tell you that the peasant boys in Cuba, those kids out in the fields, eat raw sugar cane and they have perfect teeth. What they don't tell you is that they develop rickets.

"Look at me, Ma. No cavities! But I can't walk too straight."

Another health-food delicacy is called mandrake roots. If you eat it, you're a magician. You never knew such a smell. My wife says Indians eat this. Maybe that's why they ship them out to reservations.

And you know how they fool you with names. "Zeus Smoked Zip!" Do you know what that is? Epsom salts. Or how about "Elijah Manna"? Sounds like a hotel in the mountains. Give up? It's cornflakes.

Here's my favorite—Helianthus—$1.60 a pound. You'll

never guess, but ask your kid. It's polly seeds. You go into a candy store, put a penny in a machine, you got enough for a month. With them, it's $1.60 a pound.

Oh, but wait a minute. You haven't heard anything yet. They've got things called "garlic pearls." They're supposed to be good for your blood. Maybe it's good for your blood, but it doesn't do a thing for your social life.

After you eat all this, you can wash it down with tiger's milk. So help me, that's the truth. Tiger's milk. I don't know too much about the product, but I'd just like to meet the guy who does the milking. I'd like to find out what he eats. That's going to become my diet.

They've got a cure for everything. According to their claims, you can eat your way out of any illness—high blood pressure, insomnia, coughing, head colds, even arthritis. Mayo Clinic hasn't found a cure for arthritis, but there's this nut on 8th Avenue; five years ago he had a delicatessen, but now he's a doctor of nutrition. He found a cure for arthritis. Vinegar and honey. You mix it together, stand on one leg, spit at the sun after a full moon, accompanied by a voodoo drum—and all your aches and pains go away. Who knows?

Are you tired, sluggish, run down? They've got just the thing. You should drink "Heall-All-Sea." It's water from the ocean. They've got a big plant in Coney Island. Every day, some scientist takes a bottle, picks up his pants, walks into the water, and fills it up.

Now right on the bottle it says "Dehydrated Sea Water." You know what dehydrating is. It's removing the water from something. So these geniuses, they're taking the water out of water. Six dollars a bottle.

Did you ever go into a health-food restaurant? They've got 372 of them in Manhattan, and, if you want some laughs, you should try any one. Jeanette talked me into it last week.

Well, if you are like me, when I walk into a food store, I want to have a little atmosphere—an appetizing aroma, a salami hanging in the window, a piece of white fish, a nice pink lox. These places look like hospitals.

You go in to eat, and you feel like an outpatient. The help walks around in the crisp white coats, space shoes, and they all wear long white gloves. They don't want to get blackstrap molasses on their hands. They have a scrub nurse in the back peeling potatoes, and the waiter takes your order on a prescription pad.

Our waiter came over to us, gave a little dry cough, and asked, "What can I do for you today?"

"You can turn the other way," I suggested.

You ought to see what they serve in these places. Nothing is what it's supposed to be. Wheat-germ burgers, soyaberry shortcake. They had flowers on the table. I didn't know if it was a centerpiece or my main dish. You've got to watch yourself at all times. In a health-food restaurant, if you say "hey" to a waiter, he brings it.

Probably the thing that annoys me most about health foods is that I firmly believe that your health should be a matter of concern between you and your physician. Unfortunately, it's an area that too many people neglect. We dissipate all our lives, and, when we reach the twilight zone, we all want to go back and do it over the right way. By then it's too late, so we go out and buy a book and follow fifty cents' worth of advice from a paperback quack.

If you don't feel good, go to see a doctor. Let him tell you what to eat, and if he tells you to go to a health-food store—see another doctor.

At this point I should like to acknowledge the many letters received from doctors across the country who have written to express their support of my stand on health foods.

I would also like to express my appreciation to the medical profession and to the American Medical Association for the numerous reports and the many AMA journals they sent to me and which have been so useful in my own research and studies.

What they couldn't have known at the time was that the next chapter is all about doctors and the AMA.

CHAPTER 7

NEVER GET SICK
ON WEDNESDAYS

You HAVE TO be at least my age to remember some of
the old movies where Jean Hersholt played the role of
the dedicated country doctor. If the kids today saw any
of these films on the "Late Show," they wouldn't believe
them. They wouldn't even understand them.

Oh, how I used to love that wonderful, kindly, benevo-
lent old man. According to Hollywood, the average country doctor never went to sleep. At 3 A.M. he'd hitch the
horse to the sleigh and drive thirty miles through a blind-
ing snowstorm for a firsthand look at Dora Belle Ziffer's
acne.

After that he and Clem Ziffer would go out to the barn
and help the swayback plow horse deliver a new foal.
Then he'd come back to the house and explain the facts of
life to the Ziffer kids while he eased the pain in Ma Ziffer's arthritic fingers and performed an emergency ap-
pendectomy on Grandma Ziffer whether she needed it
or not.

For this he charged two dollars, but nobody ever paid
him. If the crops came in, Ma Ziffer would bake him an
elderberry pie. But "Doc"—everybody called him "Doc"
in those days—he didn't care. He'd sit and tell stories to
the Ziffer kids until seven in the morning. Then, just for
kicks, he'd stop off at the Dionne house and deliver
some quintuplets.

Boy, have things changed.

Today there are almost 275,000 doctors in the United States. Last week I woke up with a 104-degree fever, and I couldn't get one of them to make a house call.

Did you ever try to reach your doctor in the middle of the night? If it's an emergency, you call him at home, right? Forget it. This selfless and dedicated guardian of the nation's health has an unlisted phone number.

I keep hearing how a doctor spends three times longer in training than any other professional. I'm impressed. When I'm sick, I want the benefit of all this training. I call my doctor for his great knowledge and experience.

What do you think I get? I get a telephone answering service.

I've got to talk to some broad who couldn't point to her own ribs. She's got two clients, a bookie and my doctor. She's been taking the doctor's messages for fifteen years and giving them all to the bookie. Tomorrow I've got "Sore Throat" in the fifth at Hialeah. Two years ago I had hemorrhoids, and they paid $8.80.

The phone always rings three times. That's the signal to the answering service to take over.

"Dr. Hauser's office."

Who's she kidding? It's three o'clock in the morning. She wouldn't know Dr. Hauser's office from Mount Rushmore.

"Is the doctor in?"

What the hell! I'm never too sick to play games.

"I'm sorry. The doctor is out. Can I take a message?"

"This is Mr. King, I'd like the doctor to make a house call."

"Why would you like the doctor to make a house call, Mr. King?"

"I CAN'T GO TO SLEEP. I WANTED HIM TO COME OVER AND SING 'LIEBERSTRAUM'!"

I had a sore throat, chills, and a ringing in my ears. From 3 A.M. to 4 A.M. I called every doctor in the phone book, including dentists, psychiatrists, two columns of veterinarians, and a man named Irving Doktor.

Irving Doktor turned out to be a plumber. *He* was willing to come out and look at me. Three in the morning

73

you can get Roto Rooter to unclog your sewer, but you can't find a doctor who will even talk to you.

From 4 A.M. to 7 A.M. I moaned and groaned and did everything possible to keep Jeanette awake and make her miserable, too. I don't suffer very nicely. When I get sick, I'm just like any other man.

Men can fight wars, embark on crusades, endure countless tortures, battle wild beasts, lift 500-pound weights, conquer mountains, and tame the savage fury of a hurricane. But did you ever see a man get up in the morning with a case of cramps?

"I'm sick! Boy, am I sick! Oh, boy, am I sick!"

Then he discovers that his temperature has soared to 99.3 degrees. This he determines by putting his hand on his forehead.

"I'm burning up. Bring juices. Bring aspirin."

Now his wife is hysterical, and when Richard the Lion-Hearted finds out that he not only gets his juices and his aspirin, but he gets them in a hurry, he suddenly realizes that he's got a good thing going for him. Maybe it isn't just cramps. Maybe it's something more serious. Well, if he's gotta go, he's going like a man.

"I DIDN'T SAY I WANTED ORANGE JUICE. I WANT STRAWBERRY JUICE . . .

"TELL THOSE KIDS TO BE QUIET . . .

"OPEN THE WINDOW . . .

"SHUT THE WINDOW . . .

"I WANNA SLEEP . . .

"FLUFF UP THE PILLOW . . .

"TUCK ME IN . . .

"I WANT MY MOTHER . . .

"WHERE THE HELL IS THE DOCTOR?"

I can handle things I can see and understand. But when a little bug crawls inside me and gums up the works, I fall apart.

At 7 A.M., Dr. Zimmerman rang our doorbell. He was covering for Dr. Hauser, who spent every Wednesday at the clinic. Did you ever try to get a doctor anywhere in the world on Wednesdays? Wednesdays they become the Untouchables. Every Wednesday they operate out of a sand trap.

"I'll have a number-9 scalpel, Caddy."

Dr. Zimmerman was wearing a plaid cap, tan blazer, knickers, and cleated golf shoes. If I was dead, he could still meet Dr. Hauser on the back nine.

He stood outside my bedroom door and talked to my wife in hushed tones. I got the impression that Jeanette was describing my symptoms.

"I never saw such a big baby," she said.

So that's what was wrong with me. I was pregnant.

Dr. Zimmerman walked into the bedroom wearing his $25 bedside manner.

"Well, Mr. King," he gurgled, "we don't look so good, do we? And I don't imagine we feel so good either, do we?"

I thought I was the only one who was sick. Suddenly there was an epidemic.

Dr. Zimmerman felt my forehead. Then he excused himself and went into the bathroom to wash his hands. I followed him into the bathroom and washed my forehead.

Dr. Zimmerman put a thermometer in my mouth, and, while he was waiting, he took my pulse. This impressed me tremendously. You don't see many Mickey Mouse watches these days.

"Hmmm," said Dr. Zimmerman.

He took the thermometer out of my mouth and held it up to the light.

"Hmmm," he said again.

He thumped my chest.

"Hmmm!"

I turned to Jeanette. "Listen, dear. He's humming our song."

They never tell you what's wrong with you. All they do is "hmmm." Get two doctors together and they sound like bees swarming.

It was Zimmerman's opinion that I had a 24-hour virus. It's always a 24-hour virus, but they never tell you which 24 hours. You can lie there for a month.

He wrote out a prescription and suggested we fill it immediately at Zimmerman's Drugstore, which, by a most singular coincidence, was owned by his brother. He explained that his brother was the only one who could read his handwriting.

The medicine, Dr. Zimmerman informed us, was a new miracle drug, and he warned us that it would be very expensive.

"But then," he said, "we can't put a price tag on health, can we?"

I wondered whether he'd feel the same way if I didn't pay his bill.

As soon as he left, Jeanette ran out and picked up the prescription. She had to wait ten minutes while the pharmacist poured a box of Smith Brothers' Cough Drops into a brown glass bottle.

Now at this point I want to make it clear that I have the greatest respect for the individual doctor—a sincere, if not the most humble, kind of man. Doctors are the only people I know who can be filthy rich and holier-than-thou at the same time.

But not all doctors are Schweitzers, Sabins, and Salks. They've got a few finks practicing, too. I ought to know. My brother is a doctor. I wouldn't let him cut my nails. When he was fourteen, he was still wetting his bed. His patients wouldn't know this, but I used to sleep with him.

It so happens that my brother is a very good doctor. Last year he gave me shots for the Asian flu, and the next day I had Asian flu. He never misses.

My mother, as you might expect, is very proud of my brother. Every woman wants to see her son a doctor. Now that my brother has made it, my mother sits in his office every afternoon and talks to the patients.

"What's wrong with you, my dear?"

"I've got a pain in my back."

"What you do is take a hot compress and put it on your back. Then you apply the cups. What do you need with him?"

"Who are *you*?"

"I'm his mother. Who do you think took care of him when he was a little boy—before he learned the Latin? Who do you think took him through the impetigo and the mastoid and the swollen glands?"

She chases everybody out of his office.

And do you know what I get a big kick out of? My mother won't let my brother treat her. She won't say why, but we all know the reason. She's embarrassed to get undressed in front of her own son.

Just last week my mother developed a pain across the bridge of her nose. After a big argument and pleading and cajoling, my brother finally got her to go see a prominent eye, ear, nose, and throat specialist. I've got to tell you what happened, because I think it's very funny.

True story. This specialist probed and poked and flashed his little light into her eyes and her ears and her nose. Finally he told her: "Mrs. King, I'm afraid that all your teeth will have to come out."

So my mother took out her uppers and her lowers and handed them to him. She hasn't had her own teeth in forty years.

Mind you, this guy was a specialist, yet. Everybody is a specialist today. The general practitioner is becoming as rare as the American buffalo. All the young medical students think G.P. stands for "general pauper."

Today it's medical school, internship, residency, specialization. Medicine has become so specialized, if you've got a sty, you don't go to an eye doctor. You go to an upper-right-lid man.

The AMA encourages this kind of specialization, and the AMA is a very powerful organization. It's sort of the doctors' union, only they don't call it a union. Once you graduate medical school, it don't look nice you should belong to a union. So they call it an association.

You don't have to belong to the association, but it helps. In fact, I'd like to see you go into business without it. They cut off your iodine supply. You can't even buy a tongue depressor; you've got to use your finger.

Once a year the association holds a national convention. All the doctors get together and operate on each other. They discuss things like medical ethics. "When you leave a forceps inside the patient, should you charge him for it or knock it off your income tax?"

The AMA has certainly done a lot to elevate the image of the American doctor. Now television and the movies have taken over and they've just about made him a saint.

What I can't understand is why all these big medical epics concentrate on only half of the doctor's professional life.

Whenever you see medicine dramatized, it's always the operating room—scalpel, sutures, clamps, sweat, life, death. But that's child's play. All the real drama takes place in the doctor's office.

Did you ever sit for two hours in a doctor's waiting room with nothing else to do but look through medical magazines? He puts out all his old professional journals. After three visits, you don't need him anymore. You can hang up your own shingle. I read these magazines, and I don't understand a word they're saying; but I've got to admit that the pictures absolutely hypnotize me.

There's always a two-page, full-color photograph of a polyp in somebody's nose, a black-and-white enlargement of a wart, and a "before" and "after" advertisement which illustrates a product that shrinks piles without surgery. I didn't feel too good when I walked into the office. By this time I'm violently ill. Now the doctor is ready for me.

In the specialist's office, when you get an examination, you never see the doctor until the end. He's the headliner. The nurse takes you through the obstacle course.

"Will you get undressed, Mr. King?"

"Here in the waiting room? This is what they must mean by socialized medicine."

"Please go into room A, take off your clothes, and put on this examining gown."

Did you ever examine one of these gowns they give you? They're beautiful. They're made out of the most expensive material, cheesecloth. With the two little bows. The minute you put it on you feel like an idiot. They don't have pockets in them. You don't know what to do with your hands. And the drafts! Always all the windows are wide open. The nurse walks around in a heavy wool sweater, and you're standing there in the cheesecloth examining gown.

As soon as I had the gown on, she came back into the room.

"Did you always have blue skin, Mr. King?"

"Not until I walked into this office. Close that goddam window and watch my complexion change."

"Do you mind sitting down, Mr. King?" she asked. "I'd like to take your case history."

"YIIIPE!"

They always sit you down on a cold leather chair. Instead of boiling the instruments, why don't they heat up the furniture?

"Did you ever have measles?

"Mumps?

"Chicken pox?

"Whooping cough?

"Asthma?

"Sinus?

"Hay fever?

"Bronchitis?

"Hoof-and-mouth disease?"

"No," I answered, "but I'd like to meet the guy who gets 100 percent on this test."

"Now, Mr. King, would you please get up on the examining table."

I think I prefer the cold leather chair. The examining table is covered with a long sheet of barber paper. It's like lying down on a piece of matzo. When you finally get up, you've got to peel it off.

Now it was time for the doctor to make his entrance. He was wearing a white coat with three buttons open at the neck. The little devil; he'd been watching television.

Right away he started with the examination. With the tests, with the test tubes, with the exhaling and the inhaling, with the jumping up and down. Next came the slapping and the punching and the smacking with the rubber hammer.

"Do you get that sticking pain all the time, Mr. King?"

"No, only when you hit me."

"Do you remember when it first started to hurt?" he asked.

"Right after you walked in here."

The nurse handed the doctor a little bottle and he handed it to me.

"Would you mind filling this up for me?"

"I'll try," I promised.

I always try, but the minute they hand me one of those

bottles my whole system reacts like I've been lost in the Sahara Desert for four months.

"Having trouble, Mr. King?"

"It might be a little easier if *she* left the room."

The doctor then proceeded to check my personal history. "Do you smoke, Mr. King?"

"Moderately."

"Well, I think you ought to give it up. It can't do you any good."

I could hardly understand what he was saying, because he was having a coughing spasm. He had cigarettes burning in three ashtrays and one in each hand. He's the only man I ever saw with nicotine stains on his forehead.

I still smoke, because I'm a fatalist. I could get hit by a car tomorrow. For every year medical science adds to your life, the automobile makers take two away.

Next came the bit with the X-rays, and this always upsets me. I stood there nude in front of the machine while the doctor put on a leather apron, goggles, and heavy gloves. Then he went into the other room to push the button. Why isn't the patient entitled to the same protection the doctor receives?

I went running after him. "Where ya going, Doc? The machine blowing up?"

He must know something.

Now the examination was over and we finally got down to brass tacks. The doctor went into his library to look up my symptoms in a back issue of *Readers' Digest*. He decided that there was really nothing wrong with me except maybe I had too much money, and he had a cure for that, too.

Well, look. You've got good doctors, bad doctors, heroes, and phonies. The family doctor is disappearing from the scene, but, as in every other business, medicine has reached the age of specialization. This may be progress, but it doesn't necessarily mean that it's right.

Today there are eye doctors and foot doctors and bladder doctors who wouldn't know what to do if your nose started to bleed. They go to school for five years to study the large intestine. I think they should take one more year and find out about the rest of the body.

I'll tell you what I resent, though. There's no profession that's cloaked in as much mystery as the medical profession. They all act like the wisdom of Solomon is locked in their heads.

When I was a kid, our family physician was Dr. Roth. He was a general practitioner. He didn't know half the medicine the doctors do today, but at least he showed up.

There were eight children in my family. It made no difference which one was sick, because Dr. Roth didn't play favorites. He'd line us up shoulder to shoulder. Then he'd walk up and down feeling our foreheads. Back in ancient times this was known as the "king's evil." It was the laying on of the hands. They didn't have penicillin or aureomycin in those days, or even when I was a child. But Dr. Roth could lay on with the hands and break a fever in two seconds.

If you had a swollen gland, you got your neck rubbed with Vicks and wrapped in a flannel cloth. The next day everything was fine. If you had a chest cold, you got a mustard plaster and hot milk with sugar and a pat of melted butter floating on top. Then you were buried under ten blankets while you literally sweated the cold out of your system.

And it worked. It always worked, because Dr. Roth said it would. We had confidence in that man.

The last time I had a chest cold I climbed into bed and tried to sweat it out, only now my chest specialist said I was crazy, because sweating doesn't do one bit of good. He was right. Nothing happened. And do you know why? With all their pills and miracle drugs and modern education, they've made me lose faith in Dr. Roth.

They've forgotten all about the miracles that have been wrought with just a good dose of faith and inspiration. When Dr. Roth walked into the house that little black bag could have been empty, but it didn't make any difference. We knew that everything was going to be all right, just because he was there.

My sons will never know what it's like to have a real, honest-to-goodness family doctor who treats them like his own, but I'm not so sure it matters. We've got cures for so many things today that they've had to go out and make up new diseases. That's fine for the younger generation. As for me, it's really no fun getting sick anymore.

CHAPTER 8

ATTORNEY-IN-LAW

I'M NOT TOO crazy about lawyers.

Now I don't think it's right to make a blanket condemnation of any profession, but you should understand that in the last three years I've been sued eleven times for statements I've made on television. Believe me, I've had my share of lawyers and I know more than a little bit about the law.

The nicest thing I can say about all my legal encounters is that I worked for a television network that always came up with the lawyer. They got me the district attorney from the Perry Mason show, and you know how many cases he's won.

Life is getting so complicated that you can't make a move anymore without a lawyer. They're like doctors. Everyone's a specialist, and when they don't know the answer, they start talking to you in Latin. Right away you can be sure of three things. Number one: you're in trouble. Number two: it's going to cost you a bundle. Number three: your bill will be in English.

Today you can go out and hire a trial lawyer or an estate lawyer or a realty lawyer or a will lawyer. Up until a year ago I never heard of a will lawyer, because I had never made out a will. No particular reason. I just never got around to it. I once told this to an attorney, and on the spot he broke out in hives.

"Alan, are you crazy? Do you realize that, if you don't have a will, you can die intestate?"

They scare the hell out of you with the big words. I just found out what it means to "die intestate." It means you die without leaving a will. What he was telling me was, if I die without leaving a will, I'm going to die without leaving a will. That legal pearl cost me $500.

I had a distant uncle who was an oil tycoon. When he died, he left $18 million in six trust funds and endowed a hospital and three universities. He wrote his will on the back of an envelope and had it witnessed by two ladies of the night from the local house of ill repute. No one even questioned it.

Me? I've got a lawyer and a will that runs nineteen pages. That's five more pages than the Magna Charta, but it's very important that I cover every eventuality. For example, if I drop dead outright, I'm in good shape. If I should linger awhile, I can screw up the whole works. For this they've got a standard antilingering clause. Then there's another clause that starts out, "I, Alan King, being of sound mind . . ." My lawyer insisted I put that in. I've got a sneaking suspicion that I left all my money to him.

What he doesn't know is that I've made out a new will. I've bequeathed my wife the key to the safe-deposit box and a Ouija board just in case she has any questions.

I remember the days when you used to make an agreement with someone just by shaking his hand. It was more binding than any written contract, because nobody ever sat down and tried to figure out the loopholes in a handshake. That's no good anymore. Today you've got to go to a lawyer who does nothing else but draw up contracts.

But it isn't that simple. If you don't trust the other person, he doesn't trust you either, so he's got a lawyer, too. Immediately his lawyer and your lawyer get together and have a ball. They start writing.

"The party of the first part agrees to reimburse the party of the second part for services rendered by the party of the third part to the party of the second part."

You know who's paying for this party, don't you? You are! And you're not even invited.

They've got corporation lawyers; they've got tax lawyers, criminal lawyers, trial lawyers. The lawyers, they've got lawyers. And if you've got problems with your wife, there's a lawyer for that, too. This one handles nothing but divorce actions.

"Let's not be hasty, Mr. Withersnipe. I'd rather save a marriage than earn a legal fee."

"But my wife always burns the toast."

"That's different. Heaven knows, I tried."

All other professions are making tremendous strides forward. Doctors are probing the secrets of life. Scientists are probing the secrets of the universe. You walk into a lawyer's office, and the shelves are lined with hundreds of volumes of legal precedents, case histories, and dust. Dust is a very big thing in law offices. They spread it around to remind you that the law is as old as mankind itself. Many of our laws today are derived from English common law from as far back as the sixth century. Lawyers are very proud of this. No one ever told them that this is one of the reasons we fought a revolution.

To complete the office atmosphere, all the furniture is two hundred years old, and the whole place is decorated in Contemporary Mildew. Of course there's the inevitable diploma. They not only have to go to school for six years, but once they graduate they still have to pass a stiff bar exam. By the time a lawyer is admitted to practice, he knows all there is to know about everything except the answer to a direct question.

"Well, now, Mr. King. I'm not saying 'yes' and I'm not saying 'no.' In the case of *Kravitz* vs. *Illinois,* the court ruled *nolo contendere*."

That's fine. They hung Kravitz because he didn't know what the hell they were talking about either. Lawyers can tell you anything you want to hear about *Doe* vs. *Doe, Jones* vs. *Jones,* and *Louis* vs. *Schmeling*. When it comes to your case, they're a little bit hazy.

"There are certain risks involved, Mr. King. I believe we're on safe ground, but there's always an outside chance that you could get hurt."

I love that. It's always "WE'RE" on safe ground, but "YOU" could get hurt. And he's right. I've never heard of a lawyer who went to the electric chair because he advised a client to plead guilty. It's like the tax expert. He fills out your form. He shows you where to cut corners. He notarizes your return. He sends it in to the government. The government sends you to jail.

There's something you should know. The law is not like you see it practiced on "The Defenders." They're not all E. G. Marshalls. Let me tell you a true story. I once asked a famous judge how he arrived at his decisions. Do you know what he told me?

"I listen to the plaintiff and form an opinion."

"Don't you listen to the defendant?" I asked.

"I used to," he said, "but it gets me all mixed up."

When I was growing up I had the great American dream that the man who worked eighteen hours a day, built a better mousetrap, and invested his money wisely could become wealthy. Today you can do the same thing without any of the strain or the pain. Today, if you want to get rich fast, you go out and find *somebody else* who worked eighteen hours a day, built a better mousetrap, and invested his money wisely. Then you sue him!

What are you going to sue him for? What the hell do you care? You sue him because he's got one brown eye and one blue eye. You make a big stink about something, and then you settle out of court.

That's a fact. This country is going lawsuit crazy. My neighbor down the block. I met him on the street.

"Hiya, George. How are the kids?"

"Kids? Kids are young goats. That's defamation of character, King. You'll hear from my attorney."

Even if you never get sued in your life, you've still got to pay through the nose. Who can take chances? I'm an entertainer, so it costs me $2,000 a year for libel insurance. It's also my good fortune to own a little nest in suburbia that's nothing more than a legal booby trap. For this my brother-in-law sold me another policy for $400.

"How can I be negligent in my own house? A man's home is his castle."

"You don't understand, Alan. Suppose someone slips

on your icy sidewalk. Or, worse, yet, suppose your dog bites somebody. A jury could break you overnight."

He was right. I'm glad he talked me into it. As soon as he left the house, he slipped on the ice. While he was lying there, my dog ran out and bit him. The case comes up next month.

My brother-in-law also sold me the policy on my car. I've got $300,000 liability coverage. I couldn't do $300,000 worth of damage if I drove eighty miles an hour blindfolded through the Louvre. In New York State, though, liability insurance is compulsory, and there's always some wise guy with a new angle. Just the other day I scraped the side of a parked car. The driver wasn't even in it, but he came running out of a drugstore. Right away he started complaining about migraine headaches and low back pains.

Nine o'clock the next morning his lawyer was in my office waving an X ray around in the air.

"Mr. King," he said, "my client was so upset by your accident that he's developed a very serious ulcer."

"Gee, that was sort of fast, wasn't it?"

"The doctor says it's a very unusual case."

"I think you've got a very unusual doctor."

"Nevertheless, Mr. King, we intend to sue."

"I don't blame you," I said, pointing to a dark spot on the X rays; "that's a nasty-looking ulcer."

"I'm glad you understand."

"It's dangerously close to your client's ovaries."

"Sir?"

"I said I think your client is going to have a baby."

"There's been a terrible mistake," he apologized as he backed toward the door. "Why don't we just forget the whole thing?"

"Good idea. Let me know when he gives birth so I can light a candle."

It was a great bluff. I wouldn't know an X ray from a xylophone.

I really don't understand it. Everybody is suing me like it was some kind of status symbol. I think I should get a turn, too. Last February I got clobbered by a guy who ran his car through a red light. You never saw such a mess in your life. I had a brand-new automobile that I just drove out of the dealer's showroom. Suddenly I was the proud owner of a two-wheeler. The back half was in a department-store window.

The guy who hit me? Not a scratch. He was driving a 1928 Kissel. I could have sued him for every penny he had, and I wouldn't get enough money to put air in my two good tires. He was an unemployed gypsy palm reader. He never heard of liability insurance, but he told me I was going to take a long trip with a mysterious brunette.

All my life I've initiated only one lawsuit, but I've got to admit that that one was a honey. It all started last year when I had what could have been a very serious accident. I fell off a stage. Now even for an actor, falling off a stage is not what you'd call an occupational hazard, so that requires some explanation.

What happened was I gave a benefit performance in the Grand Ballroom of a brand-new hotel in New York. When I finished my own part of the show, I introduced the next act.

"And now, ladies and gentlemen, it's my pleasure to introduce one of the finest young dance teams . . ."

The houselights were dimmed, the stage was darkened, and the dance team came on in a blackout. I went off the same way. While I was making the introduction, the stagehands decided it would be a good idea to remove the stairs. They wanted to keep them clean for an affair next week. I walked over to where the stairs were supposed to be and fell six feet.

You've gotta picture this. The band is playing "Beautiful Ohio." I'm stretched out flat on my back on the floor with a broken leg. The louder I yell for help, the louder they play. There are 2,000 people in the ballroom. Nobody heard me fall. Nobody heard me screaming and moaning—except one man. A lawyer. He was at a party in another room. His ears are attuned. He could hear an accident in another town. Right away he rushed in and the first bit of advice he gave me was, "DON'T GET UP!"

"I won't be able to unless you get your foot off my throat."

Two o'clock in the morning they rushed me to the

hospital in an ambulance. I was in a brand-new tuxedo and the first stages of shock. The emergency doctor was standing there with oxygen, plasma, and his surgical scissors.

The first thing he asked me was, "Aren't you Alan King? Aren't you the guy who does the routine on doctors?"

Right away he took the scissors and cut the pants right up the side. For all he knew, I could have been an emergency tonsillectomy.

"WHAT THE HELL ARE YOU CUTTING? I'M IN NO HURRY. I COULD HAVE TAKEN THE PANTS OFF."

"I've gotta examine the leg," he said.

"That's fine. I understand. WHY DON'T YOU LOOK AT THE LEG THAT WAS HURT?"

"You're being very difficult, Mr. King."

"Don't get me wrong, Doctor. I just thought you should cut the pants the other way. I've always wanted a pair of formal Bermuda shorts."

The next step was to take X rays. As soon as they were developed, the doctor handed them to me. "What do you think?" he asked. He couldn't read them either.

"Stunning," I said. "I'll take six of each pose for my new book, *Inside Alan King*."

Actually, nothing was broken. I had ripped a few tendons and torn a muscle. "You're a very lucky man," the doctor informed me.

"I sure am. You could have cut up the whole jacket."

While all this was going on somebody had phoned Jeanette, and she came down to the hospital to pick me up. We got home at 3 A.M., and who do you think was waiting for me at the door? My brother-in-law. You know, the one who sold me all of the insurance. He also sells mutual funds, real estate, and does tax returns. On top of this, he's a graduate lawyer. He can do everything but support his family.

To give you an idea of what a brilliant attorney he is, if he had been handling Mrs. Richard Burton, she would have ended up paying alimony to Elizabeth Taylor. He's not only a great lawyer, he's a great detective. In five different cases he uncovered last-minute evidence to prove the condemned man was innocent, and in each instance he managed to reach the governor within seconds after his client was hanged.

So now my brother-in-law was standing at the door, pouting. "You had an accident and you couldn't call me?"

"To tell you the truth, they didn't have a telephone in the ambulance. What are you doing here, anyway?"

"I called him," Jeanette volunteered. "After all, Alan, we do need a good lawyer."

"A good lawyer? He couldn't defend Ben-Gurion in Israel."

My brother-in-law doesn't insult easily. "Look here, Alan. What happened when you got a fifteen-dollar ticket for parking in a bus stop?"

"What happened? I'll tell you what happened. You told the judge I was temporarily insane, and he took away my license."

"Well, you can't win 'em all," he philosophized.

As the saying goes, blood is thicker than water, so I decided to give the case to my brother-in-law. I decided? My wife decided that I decided.

Now my brother-in-law happens to belong to a very big law firm. They have eighty names on the door. That's in case business gets slow; they can sue each other. The name of the firm is Lombardi, Kelly, Wilson, and Schwartz. They've got every parish covered. And on the bottom is my brother-in-law's name—in chalk. Him they're not too sure of.

A good way of telling a successful lawyer is by the size of the stuffed fish he's got hanging on the wall. The bigger the fish, the bigger the fee. My brother-in-law had a killer whale. Right away, he started to discuss the case in his best legal manner—my brother-in-law, the Clarence Darrow from Levittown.

"Alan, do you realize that we have the perfect open-and-shut case? We're going to sue that hotel for every penny they've got."

"I just twisted my leg."

"Just twisted? Do you realize that this injury may be permanent and lasting?"

"But I only scratched my . . ."

He put his finger to his lips to silence me. "Shhhh," he whispered. "Don't you know that there are no scratches in law? Cuts and bruises are lacerations, contusions and abrasions. A black-an-blue mark is hemotoma. We're going to sue them for $250,000."

"$250,000? I JUST HURT MY KNEE."

"Alan," he asked with a sympathetic expression on his face, "don't I know about pain? What about my football injury?"

Football injury? He fell off a barstool watching the Army-Navy game.

"WHAT, ARE YOU MAKING A FEDERAL CASE? A QUARTER OF A MILLION DOLLARS!"

"Do you realize," he cried, "that my sister—your wife—has been deprived of a sound and healthy husband?"

That did it. He just blew the whole case. I'd be lucky if my wife didn't testify for the other side. She wasn't too crazy about me when I was well.

He continued. "Do you realize that we're going to sue these people for carelessness, recklessness, and negligence?"

"And see if they'll throw in a few bucks for the torn tuxedo."

Let me tell you something. My brother-in-law was beginning to get to me. He actually had me convinced. "Pray tell, barrister," I queried, "what's in it for you? What is your fee?"

"That's simple. We lawyers all have the same procedure. If we lose, I get nothing. And if we win, you get nothing."

"That sounds fair."

It was all settled. I was practically a rich man. The first thing my brother-in-law did was call the opposition lawyer to announce his intentions.

"George, baby," he chortled, "this is Murray. How you doin' there, old pal?"

"GEORGE, BABY? OLD PAL?" I exploded. "WHAT THE HELL ARE WE DOING, SUING THEM OR ASKING FOR A DONATION?"

He put his hand over the mouthpiece. "Alan, will you

keep quiet? I went to law school with George. Do you want me to insult him?"

"How about a little hate?"

When he hung up the phone he was beaming. "We've got 'em scared now, Alan. They're going to countersue."

"That's very reassuring. For a while there I was beginning to have my doubts."

"Don't you worry." He stood up and pointed his finger toward the sky. "We'll take this case all the way up to the highest court in the land even if it breaks you."

That was last year, but I didn't hear another word about the case until four weeks ago. My brother-in-law called me all excited. "Alan, did I tell you I'd handle everything? Be in my office in an hour."

I ran down; I jumped in a cab; I went flying into his office. I had visions of $250,000.

"Alan, I threw out the bait and we got our first nibble. They want to settle out of court."

"HOW MUCH? HOW MUCH?"

"Seventy-two dollars."

"I don't think I heard you."

"Seventy-two dollars. I think we ought to take it."

"TAKE IT? WHAT HAPPENED TO THE CONSCIOUS PAIN AND SUFFERING, MENTAL ANGUISH AND SHOCK, SINIVITIS, CAUSING INFLAMMATION OF THE LEG REQUIRING IMMOBILIZATION?"

"Alan," he said piously, "you only hurt your knee."

CHAPTER 9

212-555-1212

THE TELEPHONE was invented by Alexander Graham Bell, an American, in 1876. The first message to be transmitted over a telephone was a call for help from Bell to an assistant working two floors below.

Thirty seconds later Bell received his first call. It was from his mother-in-law.

"Hello, Alex. I understand you just invented the telephone. Let me talk to my daughter."

That was the last time Bell ever talked on the phone. He couldn't get his wife off the line. He never had a chance to use it again.

Try to imagine what life would be like without the telephone. Think of what it has meant to the development of our civilization. Do you know that you can lift the receiver of this miraculous instrument and within minutes you can be talking to someone 3,000 miles away? It can be a little discouraging, of course, if you were just calling the corner drugstore.

That kind of situation can happen every now and then, because there are so many phones in the country they're running out of numbers. The whole concept of the telephone has changed.

There used to be sort of a happy rapport between the telephone and the people who used it. When I was a kid I'd pick up the phone and an operator at the other end would say, "Number, please?" You could talk to this woman, and she'd answer back. You could ask her a question, and she'd give you an answer. I'd tell her, "Get me Main 6015," and she'd get it for me.

But they don't have operators anymore. Every phone is a dial telephone, and they call that progress. We've turned into the first generation of Americans whose index fingers are shorter than their thumbs. Instead of an operator, everything is a record.

"This is a recorded announcement. The number you have reached is not a working number. Would you please hang up and . . ."

"This is a recorded announcement. When dialing Nassau County, use the area code 516 and . . ."

"This is a recorded announcement. The circuits are all busy. Please hang up and . . ."

The telephone company is going out of business. It's gonna come back as an album. They've automated the whole works. The only human beings in the entire company are the musicians on the Bell Telephone Hour.

They've even got a special service when you dial a number and hear a recorded announcement that gives you the latest weather report. I call it three times a day just to hear the voice of a woman who isn't yelling at me.

My sweet little mother doesn't know from recordings. She only remembers the time when she called all of the operators by their first names. She can't understand the dial phone. She's always making mistakes and getting some kind of recorded announcement, but she thinks it's a real person.

Well, you and I know if you don't hang up the announcement will be repeated until you do. But my mother thinks it's unpardonably rude to hang up without saying "good-by" to the person you're talking to. She can stand there for hours.

But that's not all about the telephone that has changed. All the prefixes used to have such lovely sounding names —like Evergreen and Whippoorwill and Forsythia and Magnolia. Do you know what my prefix is now? 598! That's right. I just received a notice that my new number is 598-6015. I can't even remember my wife's birthday so how the hell am I supposed to remember a number like that?

The telephone company calls this ANC, which stands for "All Number Calling." And, believe it or not, there's a group of people out in California who have formed the "Anti-Digit Dialing Society." They're actively opposed to ANC on the ground that it dehumanizes the daily business of telephone calling. I wish them all the luck in the world.

While they're crusading, there's another winner I'd like to see them dig their teeth into. If I'm at the office, and I want to call home, the first thing I must dial is 516. This is my area code number. Every section of the country has one. You don't have to call the long-distance operator. You can dial direct.

The other day I called my barber and forgot to include his area code. I ended up on the White House hot line. Before I could say I was sorry, three squadrons from the Strategic Air Command penetrated five miles into Russia.

Jeanette called her sister last month. When we got the bill we found out that she had been talking for forty-five minutes to a Chinese hand laundry in Honolulu.

This whole-numbers bit is going from the ridiculous to the sublime. For example, have you tried to get Information recently?

In New York the number used to be 411. I was in Europe and never knew they had changed the system. They waited until I got out of the country. When I returned, I tried to call a friend of mine from the airport. First I called Information.

Now I'm not too crazy about the telephone operators who are still left. I don't think they care about their work. For $1.25 an hour I don't expect them to take vows, but at least they could do the basic job they're hired for.

"Operator," I said, "would you give me the number of Sam Schreiber, 124 East 3rd St.?"

"You can find that listed in your directory," she replied.

"Excuse me, lady, You happen to be busy? You have another job? You climbing poles? Stringing wires, maybe?

Would you mind looking the number up for me? I happen to be illiterate."

"The number is 399-7971. In the future, when dialing Information, please use your area code of 212 for Manhattan. For nationwide information, refer to 555-1212."

That's great. Now I forgot Sam Schreiber's number.

Did you ever see a New York phone book? Go find a number. If you can lift it, you automatically qualify for the United States Olympic Team. And that's just the regular directory. The classified book is the same deal all over again.

They've got a big campaign on to educate people to use the classified directory. They keep telling you, "Let your fingers do the walking through the Yellow Pages." They've got a little jingle they sing while two fingers walk up and down the television screen. It's the sort of thing that can shake you up pretty good.

I've got a brother-in-law who hasn't had the price of a bus ride in fifteen years. He lets his fingers do the walking. He goes down a line of pay phones and shoves his fingers up the coin return slots. The sneaky type.

Me? Not only don't I find money, but I never get my dime back. Now I've got to call the operator again.

"Operator, my call wasn't completed and I didn't receive my coin back."

"Well, if you'll give me your name and address, we'll be happy to mail you ten cents in stamps."

"Lady, I don't need stamps. I don't want to start a correspondence with you. I've got enough pen pals."

Do you know how to get even with the operator when she pulls that routine on you? I've got it all worked out. If she won't give you the dime back, you say, "All right, will you get me my number please?"

She'll say, "Please deposit a dime."

But you don't deposit a damn thing. You just wait. Then she says, "I'm sorry, but I didn't hear the coin drop."

"I PUSHED IN TEN CENTS' WORTH OF STAMPS. SEE HOW YOU LIKE IT!"

There are more than eighty million telephones in the United States today. Almost every one of them is owned by or connected with an organization called A.T.&T., the

American Telephone and Telegraph Company, which is a part of the Bell Telephone System. It's quite a business. Although I have a few misgivings about the telephone itself, I have nothing but the highest regard for A.T.&.T. You've got to agree, it's one of the finest monopolies in the world.

Of course, if you don't like the service you're getting from A.T.&.T. you can always hire yourself another company. There are three Indians in Utah who relay smoke signals.

With all these phones in the country, have you ever thought of going to your local department store to buy one? Of course not. You don't buy a telephone; you rent it, and, by happy coincidence, this, too, is done through your friendly telephone company. You can't even build a telephone pole with your own tree.

Our home had nine phones when we bought it. My wife was all excited. It was like having her mother in every room. The day we moved in, a man from the telephone company came over and took every one of the phones out. Obviously there was a mistake. Somebody was confused. I found out it was me.

Both Jeanette and I assumed he was there to test the line or change the dial. Maybe he was stringing wires in our neighborhood and just wanted to use the bathroom. When he began to unscrew the wall phone from a kitchen cabinet, I got a little curious.

"Sir," I asked with all due respect and deference, "can you tell me what you're doing?"

"Taking out your telephones, Mac," he replied without looking at me.

"Oh, good. I was afraid we were in the path of the Transatlantic Cable."

He got on his hands and knees and began to cut wires that ran along the baseboard. One of these wires belonged to the toaster. I decided to try again.

"Look, I think I can save you a lot of trouble. My wife and I have decided that we want to keep all the phones."

"Gotta come out, Mac," he grunted, cutting the wire to the electric can opener.

I got down on the floor with him. "Look, pal," I pleaded,

"we not only want all nine phones, we want them just exactly where they are. You don't have to change a thing."

"No good, Mac. Phones come out. You want phones, you call the company. They send a man. He puts the phones in."

I shrugged my shoulders. I wasn't going to get upset because he was taking out all my phones. I was grateful he didn't come from the Department of Sanitation.

Actually, there's a good reason for replacing old telephones with new ones. They keep changing the equipment so fast, it's the only way a person can keep up with the latest developments.

Like the man said, I called the company.

"What color would you like, Mr. King? They come in six delicious flavors. Would you like a wall phone, table model, intercom system, push button? Perhaps you would like our Princess model?"

"I just want a plain phone that you talk on one side and hear on the other side. It should ring."

"What type of ring would you like, Mr. King? Would you like a bell, buzzer, or chime?"

"How about two choruses of Jeanette MacDonald singing 'When I'm Calling You'?"

I left the selection to my wife, and she came up with a chartreuse phone that hums.

We settled for two phones and fourteen extensions. With an extension, you don't need a telephone in every room. They give you a phone with an extension plug, and you carry it around with you. We were in our new house for two weeks when we found out how practical that was.

The phone started ringing at three o'clock in the morning. I'm sure that it has happened to everyone. It scares the blazes out of you. Jeanette wouldn't even answer. Right away she started to cry. I was a little nervous, too.

"Alan, the phone is ringing."

"What phone? I don't hear any phone."

"Listen," she wailed. "I think it's the phone in the den."

"We don't have a phone in the den."

"You're right. I think it's in the playroom."

"We don't have a playroom."

"I don't care what you say, Alan. There's a phone ringing in this house."

We've got a clock in our bedroom with an alarm that can crack plaster. Every morning it goes off in my wife's ear and she doesn't twitch. We've got a phone in the basement that doesn't even have a bell. It has a light that blinks on and off. That she can hear.

To complicate things, we've got a brown phone in the brown room, a white phone in the white room, and a green phone in the green room. This is so they blend in with the decor. They blend in so well that, when the phone rings, you can't find it.

"Plug in the extension phone," she pleaded.

"Okay. Where is it?"

"I can't remember where I put it," she replied.

There is a rather interesting situation. We've got a ten-room house and fourteen phone outlets. They had to put two of them in the broom closet. Now my wife can't remember where she left the telephone.

I finally found it in the stall shower. I plugged it into a jack on the back of the bathtub and put the receiver to my ear just in time to hear the party at the other end hang up. Before the night was over this happened three more times. At seven in the morning I made a phone call of my own. I called the telephone company supervisor.

"Operator," I said, "this is Alan King. Someone keeps calling my house at all hours of the night and then hangs up."

"Don't worry, Mr. King," she reassured me. "It was probably just some crackpot."

"SO WAS THE GUY WHO ASSASSINATED LINCOLN!"

The telephone is no longer an instrument of communication. Not even counting the midnight calls, it has become an instrument of torture. You could drive my wife stark, raving mad by locking her in a room with a phone that's out of order.

She's on the telephone morning, noon, and night. My kids honestly believe that their mother's face consists of two eyes, a nose, and a big black thing that hangs out of one ear. And while she's talking on the phone, she can open the door, dust the house, and cook dinner with her feet.

For a few extra dollars she got a fifty-foot extension cord that reaches every room in the house. When she calls me at the office, I never know which room she's talking from. I'm afraid to ask, but sometimes my imagination gets the better of me.

For the distinction of being a link in the Bell Telephone System, I receive a monthly bill that looks like the annual report from the Bank of America. I don't want to deny Jeanette her greatest pleasure in life, but for the same money I could buy her the National Broadcasting Company.

Last summer we shipped the boys to camp, closed down the house, and Jeanette and I took off for two glorious months in Europe. I was ecstatic. With Jeanette away from the telephone, I'd save money no matter what the trip cost me. That's what I thought. I forgot about transcontinental phone calls. My wife spent so much time calling her mother and sister that the State Department used to break in and ask her to get off the line.

When we got home we still had a forty-dollar phone bill. It was obviously a mistake, and I relished the thought that for once I was going to make the telephone company squirm. The next day I called the business office.

Let me tell you something. When you call the business office, you're getting right into the guts of the little old telephone company. Now you are playing in the major leagues. You're not talking anymore to some disgruntled operator with a stereotyped nasal twang.

Instead, they connect you with a doll who introduces herself as your personal representative. You can't insult her. No matter what kind of complaint you might have, she pants, she lilts, she purrs, she coos. It sounds like the switchboard at Polly Adler's.

My personal representative's name was Miss Fleishman, and she was breathing so heavily that I had difficulty understanding her. I was having a few palpitations of my own. I explained the situation to her.

"Why, bless you," she said in sort of a hoarse

whisper. "If we made a mistake, we want to correct it. You wait right there while I get your records."

I cheated. While she was getting the records, I ran upstairs and took a cold shower.

"Hmmm," said Miss Fleishman when she returned to the phone. "Mr. King, are you SURE you were away in July and August?"

Already I was becoming disenchanted with Miss Fleishman.

"Well, now that I think of it, it might have been December and January. It's so hard to remember."

"Are you sure that nobody else used the phone, Mr. King?"

"I forgot all about that. We had a big burglary while we were gone. They didn't touch the silver or the china or the furs or the jewelry. All they did was use the telephone."

"I'll tell you what," she volunteered. "We'll put a test on your line, and I'll let you know what happens."

"A test?"

"That's right. We just want to make sure that your phone is in working order."

"WHAT DO YOU THINK I'M DOING NOW, BOUNCING THIS CALL OFF TELSTAR? THE PHONE WORKS FINE. I WANNA KNOW WHY I GOT A FORTY-DOLLAR BILL FOR LAST SUMMER?"

I still haven't heard the results of the test. I'm dying to find out if I was in Europe in July and August. If the telephone company tells me I wasn't, I've got a lot of money coming back from Pan American Airways. I don't even know what the test is all about. Miss Fleishman said something about waiting to see if the rabbit dies.

I'm not about to tell anyone what my regular monthly phone bill comes to. My wife doesn't spend much time at home, but when she does, A.T.&T. goes up anywhere from one to five points on the New York Stock Exchange. You wouldn't believe what goes over the telephone. I wouldn't have believed it either, but I was sick a short time back and had to spend the day at home. Here's a rough idea of how it went.

9:30 A.M.   Wife's mother calls. "Did *he* leave
            yet?"
            "No. *He's* sick. He's going to be here
            all day."
            "Call me back when he can't hear."

Now Jeanette begins in earnest. It's like she beds down
for the winter. She never talks on the phone sitting or
standing. She's always prone—on a bed or a sofa. Sometimes she'll just sprawl out right on the floor.

9:32 A.M.   My wife calls her sister. They arrange
            to meet for lunch. They prepare an
            agenda of what they're going to talk
            about. Sister tells Jeanette her hus-
            band swore at her. Jeanette consoles
            sister by describing what life is like
            with me. Together they decide that
            Lila Schneider is not pregnant. Just
            fat.

10:30 A.M. My wife calls her mother. Cries about
            trying to run a household on her allow-
            ance. They talk about how cheap I
            am. Mother reminds wife she warned
            her eighteen years ago.

11:00 A.M. Lila Schneider calls my wife. My wife
            tells her how well she looks. Lila tells
            Jeanette she's seven months' pregnant.
            They talk about Millie Berman's hair.

11:30 A.M. My wife's sister calls back. There's a
            sale at Hochman's Dress Shop. They
            discuss their finances. They both cry.
            They decide that if they like something
            they'll charge it.

NOON   Jeanette calls butcher and orders chick-
            en for dinner. He should deliver it.
            Before he delivers it, he should bar-
            becue it. He tells her Leona Hochman
            is ordering cheaper cuts of meat. They
            decide that Hochman's Dress Shop is
            in trouble.

102

12:15 P.M.	Wife calls sister. They discuss what they'll talk about when they meet for lunch.
12:30–3:00 P.M.	Lunch.
3:05 P.M.	Jeanette calls her sister. They analyze what they talked about at lunch.
3:15 P.M.	Jeanette calls her mother and asks her for dinner. Tells her about clothes she charged at Hochman's.
3:30 P.M.	Jeanette calls butcher and tells him to barbecue another chicken. Finds out what Rozzie Zuckerman and Harriet Schneid are having for their dinner.
3:45 P.M.	Wife calls hairdresser and makes appointment for Friday.
4:00 P.M.	Jeanette calls Rozzie Zuckerman and tells her Lila Schneider is pregnant. Rozzie wants to know how Millie Berman's hair got so yellow. They decide she must be doing it herself. She goofed on the formula.
4:30 P.M.	Harriet Stone calls Jeanette. They talk about Rozzie Zuckerman.
5:00 P.M.	Jeanette calls sister. They switch beauty-parlor appointments. Jeanette trades two barbecued chickens for one pot roast.
5:30 P.M.	Jeanette's mother calls to tell her that she'll be over in an hour. They talk for forty-five minutes.
7:00 P.M.	Jeanette's sister calls. Wants to know if she's interrupting dinner. Jeanette assures her we've just finished. Fails to mention that what we've just finished is our soup. Pot roast burns.
9:00 P.M.	Jeanette calls sister for a summary of the day's events and a late news roundup.

Mind you, now, this is the telephone schedule for one

day—when I'm home sick. What the hell goes on when I'm down at the office?

Jeanette calls me an average of twice a day. The first time is in the morning.

"I love you. I miss you terribly. Go to the bank. Bring me money."

The second time is in the afternoon. Jeanette has some sort of sixth sense. She never calls until I'm in the middle of crucial contract negotiations and my office is filled with bankers and lawyers. About this time a breathless secretary bursts into the room and announces: "Mr. King. Your wife is on the phone. SHE SAYS IT'S A MATTER OF LIFE AND DEATH!"

Everything with Jeanette is a matter of life and death. She's the only human being that the Federal Government has ever declared a disaster area.

"Hello, hello. Jeanette, my God, what's wrong?"

"I want you to tell Bobby that he can't go to Freddy Grossman's house."

"Jeanette, I'll call you back in ten minutes."

"Alan, that kid doesn't listen to a word I say. He's fresh; he's rude; he's absolutely impossible."

"Jeanette, please. I can't talk now."

"Alan, this is your child, too, you know. You *are* his father."

I'm not a jealous man, but I find that reassuring. "Okay. Put him on."

At this point I hear all sorts of garbled commotion at the other end of the line. It's Jeanette's voice that comes back to me.

"See? See what I mean? He won't even come to the phone. You think my life is a bed of roses, don't you? You think . . ."

"Jeanette, honest. I'm in the middle of an important meeting."

"Well, Alan King, I can tell what's important to you. We'll finish this discussion later."

That's swell. I just can't wait to get home. Just so the day shouldn't be a total loss, everyone in my office has been listening to this brilliant conversation. Now I've got to convince the president of the bank that I'm a sound financial risk, and he's looking at me like I'm some kind of a nut.

This kind of thing goes on all the time, and I think the telephone company encourages it. Did you ever read some of their advertisements?

"YOUR LOVED ONES ARE NEVER MORE THAN A PHONE CALL AWAY!"

It's frightening. There's no place to hide anymore. Now I know why the astronauts go up in rocket ships. They're looking for a place that's more than a phone call away.

I know dozens of businessmen who work late every night, because it's the only time they can accomplish anything. When they take a vacation, they don't think of fishing or swimming or golf. They just dream about two weeks without the incessant, demanding, nerve-shattering ring of the telephone.

I've got a theory that there's a direct relationship between the growth of the telephone industry and the increase in nervous disorders in this country. People keep telling me, "That damn telephone is driving me crazy."

Well, I've been saying this for years. We're all becoming telephone addicts. For years I've been warning that we're all going to be slaves to the most fantastic system of wires and electrical relays ever devised by man. I never thought anyone was taking me seriously, but I'm happy to say that I was wrong.

After all of the years that I've been talking about the telephone, I finally got a call from the president of the phone company. That's right. One night last week. I answered the phone. I couldn't have been more surprised.

"Mr. King, this is the president of your telephone company. It has come to my attention that you've been maligning our organization. I think you are being very unfair. In reality, sir, we're a warm, friendly, compassionate, and humane company dedicated to understanding and personal service. Perhaps this call will make you realize that we really do care."

"Mr. King, this is the president of your telephone company. It has come to my attention that you've been maligning our organization. I think you are being very unfair. In reality, sir, we're a warm, friendly, compassionate, and humane company dedicated to understanding and personal service. Perhaps this call will make you realize that we really do care."

"Mr. King, this is the president of your telephone company. It has come to my attention that you've been . . ."

CHAPTER 10

GOD REST YE,
MERRY GARBAGE MEN

> At Christmas play
> And make good cheer,
> For Christmas comes
> But once a year.
> THOMAS TUSSER (1524–1580)

I RECEIVED A Christmas card this morning that I've just got to share with the rest of the world.

It read, "Dear Mr. and Mrs. King: May the coming year be a bountiful one for you and your family. May the spirit of the Yuletide season envelop you, inspire you, and bless you."

It was signed: "Harry, Max, and Gerald, your regular sanitation men."

Now, there's real sentiment for you. Unfortunately, I wouldn't recognize Harry and Gerald if they had been the thirty-fourth and thirty-fifth presidents of the United States. Max, I know. He's the one who keeps knocking at the front door to tell me that I've got to stop mixing cans and bottles with the combustibles.

Yesterday I received a card saying, "Bless you, dear sir," from Al, Red, and Charley. Who are Al, Red, and Charley? They're Harry, Max, and Gerald's summer replacements. Three months out of the year these jokers manage to leave all my garbage-pail covers in the middle of the street. By noon they look like unidentified flying objects.

I felt very bad. Overnight I had made six new friends, and I hadn't sent any of them a Christmas card of my own. My wife, of course, had the perfect solution. "It isn't too late," she said, "to leave money."

I'm no fool. I've been through all of this before. For ten years these same guys have been strewing so much food across my lawn that my crabgrass has heartburn. But every year around this time they manage to envelop and inspire and bless me for a bountiful five bucks apiece.

"And," Jeanette added, "don't forget the milkman."

How could I forget him? He holds a second mortgage on our house.

"And the paper boy."

"That's a *boy*? He's got gray hair and a Cadillac to match."

"That's his father. He helps his son during the football season."

"Well, they've got an athletic family. The old man's been throwing the paper on our roof for a month."

Don't get me wrong. I firmly believe in the old adage that "it's better to give than to receive." It's a wonderful philosophy. Surprisingly enough, most of the people I know feel exactly the way I do—it's better Alan King should give.

About the first of December people I haven't seen all year long start knocking at my door. Last week it was the laundryman. I knew he had more than laundry on his mind, because he asked for me.

"Just thought I'd drop by, Mr. King, and wish you a very merry Christmas."

"Well, thank you, George. How about coming in for a little nip? Take the chill off your bones."

"Oh, no, thank you, Mr. King. It's really quite warm outside."

"That's nice, George. Then why don't you take your hands out of my pockets?"

Two days later it was Mr. Berger, the gardener.

"Mr. King. Just thought I'd drop by and wish you and your family a very happy Chanukah."

"Chanukah? Well, now, that's certainly very nice of you, Mr. Berger. Are you Jewish?"

"No, sir, but I'm crazy about your traditions."

I really thought Mr. Berger was sincere until he handed me the calendar. That was just what I needed. Another calendar with a chronological listing of one-cent sales at Walgreen drugstores. They all come around with the calendars. This is *their* present to *you*.

When they take the census in our town, they don't go door to door. They borrow Jeanette's Christmas list and count the names. You wouldn't believe the number of people we make happy. There are the butcher, the dry-cleaning man, our gas-station attendant, the soda-water man, the kid who washes the car, and the kid who shovels the walk.

Every year I've got to go back to our old apartment building and tip the elevator operators. My wife feels they shouldn't be deprived just because we decided to move.

Where does it all end? I don't know. I asked Jeanette the same question.

" 'Cast thy bread upon the waters,' " she replied, " 'for thou shalt find it after many days.' That's from the Old Testament, Alan."

"You can buy a loaf of bread for thirty cents. Show me the line where it says, 'Thou shalt throw thy money down the drain.' "

This year I found a new name on my wife's Christmas list. Pierre.

"Who's Pierre? Pierre who?"

"Just Pierre. That's his whole name. You know, Alan. He's the man who owns the beauty parlor. I thought I'd like to give him a little gift at Christmastime."

"I think you're a little confused. Pierre *owns* the beauty parlor. *You* are Pierre's customer. *You* don't give Pierre a gift. Pierre gives *you* a gift. Right?"

"Wrong. That's what makes it so nice, Alan. It's that warm feeling of giving something to someone instead of receiving something from someone who should be giving something to you."

Now there's real logic for you. I get the same kind of

warm feeling. It's the bank breathing down my neck. With a deal like that, Pierre can afford to give up his first name, too.

Strangely enough, in our house we seldom disagree on the people we want to remember. The problem is usually how much to give. The giving itself is easy. You go to the store or the bank and get a supply of little envelopes with holes cut ingeniously from the middle of them. Then you slip cash into an envelope so the President's picture appears in the hole. The envelope says "Merry Christmas" on it, and it makes a great gift for people who don't believe in Santa Claus but still have faith in George Washington.

As for how much to give, my wife has her own formula.

"How much shall we give to the mailman, Alan?"

"I don't know. How about three dollars?"

"Margie Abrams says she's giving him four dollars."

"So give him four dollars."

"If Margie tells me four dollars, Alan, I know very well she intends to give him five."

"So give him five dollars."

"He goes to Margie's house first. We've got to give him six dollars."

"I've got an idea. Let's buy him his own post office."

"Oh, Alan, do you really think we could?"

When I was a kid we used to give each deliveryman a jar of chocolate-chip cookies that my mother made with her own hands. The ingredients cost her fifteen cents, and the card she enclosed included a reminder to return the jar by the end of the week. Today you give the mailman a hundred shares of his favorite blue-chip stock. If you try to deduct it from your income tax, they arrest you for bribing a Federal employee.

Last night I decided that enough was enough. "Look," I pleaded. "Is there any reason we have to go in hock to thank people for doing a job they're getting paid to do?"

"Yes, Alan, there's a very good reason," she said. "It's Christmas."

"I know it's Christmas, but at this rate I won't have enough money to buy a present for you."

"If I thought that was true," she replied, "nothing you could buy me could make me happier."

Now how can you argue with a woman like that? "Jeanette," I told her, "you're very sweet, and don't you forget that I love you."

"I love you, too, Alan," she cooed, resting her head on my shoulder, "and don't you forget—"

"Yes, dear?"

"The plumber."

"I won't."

CHAPTER 11

WELCOME ABOARD,
SEE AGENT * *

THERE'S NO DENYING it, the air age is upon us.

I keep reading about the new commercial planes that they're working on now. Supersonic jets traveling three times the speed of sound—2,000 miles an hour. They'll leave New York at 9 A.M. and arrive in Los Angeles at 7 A.M. the same morning.

Figure that one out. It's like the Fountain of Youth. You take off from the East Coast a forty-year-old man and end up on the West Coast an eight-year-old boy.

All this is very impressive, I'm sure. The airplane has come a long way. Two thousand miles an hour. That's great. And you can't find a safer way to travel. The safety record of the commercial airlines is phenomenal, but we take this pretty much for granted or we wouldn't fly in the first place.

I'm no longer amazed that a plane takes off and lands. Once you accept the theory of flight, you begin to look for other things. After all, the airline business is really a service business. They all perform well in the air. It's on the ground where they screw up.

On the ground they have to depend on the human element. That's the service part of it. I happen to think that they're abusing the hell out of us.

On the ground the airlines are geared to a maximum efficiency of three people—the pilot, the copilot, and the stewardess. They've got it made. They can always get on the plane. In 10 minutes the airlines can load 150 hot meals, 4 tons of luggage, 10 tons of freight, 400 little bottles of booze. No problem. It's all automatic. But they still haven't figured out how to get the passengers on board.

It's a big joke. In New York, during the winter, one of the airlines has an advertisement on television showing some guy romping in the surf in Florida. He runs out of the water, flashes a big smile, and waves to the audience.

"Hey, up there. Why don'tcha come on down? The weather is wonderful in sunny Miami Beach. Right now it's 80 degrees. Not a cloud in the sky. The fishing and golf were never better.

"Why don'tcha hop a plane and join the fun? Just get on board a new fan jet 707, and you can be with me in less than three hours."

Do you know how *he* got down to Florida? He took a Greyhound bus. He didn't want to miss the season.

You probably think I'm exaggerating. Maybe I am a little. But let me tell you something—a true story. Three airlines fly between New York and Miami Beach—Eastern, Northeast, and National. Three weeks ago Sunday I went to Miami Beach with my wife. I was starting an engagement that night at the Eden Roc Hotel, and we were booked on Eastern Airlines Flight 11, scheduled to leave at 12:01 in the afternoon.

Now if they would say, "Around noon" or maybe "11:30," you wouldn't get so mad at them. But it's always 12:01 like somebody was going to stand out on the runway with a stopwatch.

"Ten . . . nine . . . eight . . . seven . . . six . . . five . . . four . . . three . . . two . . . one. IT'S 12:01! BLAST OFF!"

Our ticket said, "For Resort Areas, please arrive at the airport one hour before flight time," so my wife and I got to Kennedy International Airport at exactly eleven o'clock. This was no mean trick, because we were going to Florida for six days and my wife had twelve bags. I've got the wash and wear suit on a hanger, because there's no room in the twelve bags. I've got my underwear in the inside pocket and a brown paper bag with a chicken-fat stain with my socks. I'm traveling like a gypsy and she's got twelve pieces of matched luggage.

The first thing we did was to find ourselves an agent and check in. I always manage to plant myself in the shortest line and then find out that the guy in front of me is booking an around-the-world tour for the Salt Lake City Tabernacle Choir.

My turn came forty-five minutes later, and by this time I had a nervous tic in my cheek and the start of a gastric ulcer. To add to my pleasure, the agent hit me with a charge of $93 for overweight, so you can imagine how thrilled I was with the trip to begin with. I didn't know how lucky I was, because he never weighed Jeanette's purse. She had enough stuff packed away in there to open a southeast branch of Sears, Roebuck.

"Excuse me," I inquired of the agent, "but is the 12:01 on time?"

He stood there in his blue blazer with the merit badge with a tight-lipped smile on his face. They all look the same. The tight-lipped smile is to keep them from laughing in your face when you ask if the 12:01 is on time. The merit badge is for lying.

"Please check our electronic schedule board at the north end of the terminal," he advised me.

The electronic schedule board looks like the master plan for the Strategic Air Command. It flashes the times of arrival, the times of departure, and the reason that nothing's moving. All you've got to do is study the board. Everything is there, plain as day.

"FLIGHT 8—9:05—Cancelled"

"FLIGHT 40—9:18—Cancelled"

"FLIGHT 113—10:27—See Agent * * (whatever * * means)"

"FLIGHT 11—12:01—Servicing aircraft"

When they say they're "servicing aircraft" it can mean almost anything. The only thing you can be sure of is that the plane is not going to take off at 12:01. Now they start announcing the delays.

"Your attention, please. Eastern Airlines Flight 11 has been delayed for servicing. A new time of departure will be announced at 12:45."

114

Comes 12:45, the loudspeakers blare forth again.

"Your attention, please. Eastern Airlines announces that its 12:45 announcement has now been delayed approximately one hour. Departure time for Flight 11 originally scheduled to depart at 12:01 will now be announced at 1:45."

It's getting a little ridiculous. How many fights can you have with your wife? On top of the fights, it's a little disconcerting to walk over to the insurance machine and find that it's all sold out. Somebody must know something.

At 3:15 the panic sets in. I was opening that night, and it finally occurred to me that I just might not make it. I grabbed the passenger service agent—by the throat.

"I'VE GOT TO GET OUT OF HERE. WHAT'S HAPPENING TO THE 12:01?"

"Mr. King, we're still servicing the aircraft."

"IT'S FOUR HOURS. YOU'VE HAD ENOUGH TIME TO REDECORATE THE AIRCRAFT!"

"Mr. King," he said apologetically, "we're terribly sorry, but if you're smart, Northeast Airlines has a flight leaving in thirty-five minutes. We can try to get you on it."

Now they start with the phone calls like they're trying to reach the governor for the reprieve.

"Can we get two seats up front? Yes? They're holding the flight, Mr. King. Get right over."

Now I've got to try to get twelve bags back from the airline. It's tough enough when you arrive at the point of destination. But I just gave them the bags. They put them on the bill. The bags go through two doors. That's an incinerator at the other end. They burn them.

There's one thing I must explain about Kennedy International Airport in New York. If you've never been there, you have to take my word for it. It's the most impressive airport in the world. And it's unique, too, because every major airline has its own individual terminal. You can't walk from one airline to another, because all the terminals are about a quarter of a mile apart.

This can pose a problem. The cabs—those magnificent New York cabdrivers—they line up in front of each terminal for two or three hours waiting for a fare to New York City. Kennedy Airport is twenty-five miles from the heart of the city. There's going to be a five- or six-buck tab.

Already you can see the whole picture. Jeanette and I came barreling out of the Eastern Air Lines terminal, jammed twelve bags into this cab, and jumped in after them.

"NORTHEAST AIRLINES!" I shouted. "AND HURRY!"

The cabdriver didn't even turn around. I could see the back of his neck getting red.

"It's over there," he said, pointing at a building dead ahead of us.

"I know where it is. I want you to take us there."

He turned around and looked me square in the eye. "I'll lose my place in line."

I stared right back. "I tell you what. I'll mind your place in line. *You* take my wife. *You* go to Florida with her."

We got into a fistfight and a cop came over. "Take him where he wants to go," he ordered.

The whole drive took less than a minute, and the entire tab was thirty-five cents. I gave the cabbie a buck.

"If you didn't have such a big mouth," I informed him, "I'd have given you two dollars."

Actually, I never would have given him two dollars. I just wanted to aggravate him a bit.

So there we were at Northeast Airlines, and the passenger agent was waiting for us as we came tearing through the door.

"Mr. King, we're holding up the flight. Please! The last ramp up."

Now my wife in tights is not an Olympic runner. With the fur coats and the shoe boxes and the hats she had trouble standing up. Any minute she was going to collapse.

The two of us were staggering down the passageway. She's yelling, "IT'S ALL YOUR FAULT." I'm yelling, "WILL YOU COME ON ALREADY!" Over to the last ramp. Up the stairs. Into the plane. Into the seats. Fasten the safety belts. This is a great way to go to Florida. Right away I need oxygen.

Obviously this couldn't go on forever, and I'm happy to say that it didn't. Northeast Airlines was a paragon of efficiency. Jeanette and I no sooner got settled than the doors closed, and right on time the plane taxied out to the runway.

I don't know how you feel about it, but to me there is nothing more thrilling than takeoff time. This giant bird, tons of steel and aluminum, was poised and ready to vault into the heavens. The tread of the mammoth wheels gripped the runway as a surge of power coursed through one engine . . . two engines . . . three engines . . . four engines.

For forty-five minutes we sat there surging power. We didn't move an inch.

Finally the voice of the pilot came booming over the public-address system.

"Ladies and gentlemen, because of exceptionally heavy traffic conditions at Kennedy International Airport, there will be a slight delay in takeoff."

An hour and a half later we were still sitting in the same spot. They had to send a truck out so we could refuel. Finally the public-address system clicked on again.

"Ladies and gentlemen, we're next in line on the runway. We should be taking off right away. Please make certain your seat belt is securely fastened."

I tightened my seat belt another inch. Outside the plane we could hear the fan jet engines developing the thousands of pounds of thrust necessary to lift the plane off the ground. Only now there was a new sound.

"SPFFFFT, PAKOW, SPFFFT."

You don't have to be a mechanic to hear that engine spitting. A little old lady sitting in front of us turned around and timorously asked me, "What happened?"

"I think we broke our rubber band," I answered. "All I know is that we're not going to Florida."

On again came the public-address system.

"Ladies and gentlemen, because of a plunk condition in the number-two port feeder supply line controlling the left differential, it will be necessary to return to the hangar for repairs."

Then the plane taxied back to the terminal. This gave the stewardess time for one more announcement.

"Ladies and gentlemen, on behalf of your captain and

the crew, we've enjoyed having you aboard. Thank you for flying Northeast Airlines."

There we were. We had been at the airport for six and a half hours. Scott Carpenter, he went around the world already eighty-two times. We were still at Kennedy Airport.

By the time I found the passenger service agent I was in a state of blind despair.

"Look," I implored, "I've got to give a performance in exactly five hours. I MUST GET TO FLORIDA."

"Mr. King," he said, "if you're smart, Eastern Air Lines has a flight leaving in twenty minutes. I think I can get you on it."

Eastern Air Lines? The name had a familiar ring. The same flight I was originally scheduled on is now going to leave and he *thinks* he can get me on it.

Now we started with the bags again. Up the escalator. Through the lobby. Out the door and into a waiting cab. I take an oath that this is true. Who do you think we got? The same cabdriver.

"WHERE WERE YOU?"

"WHAT THE HELL BUSINESS OF YOURS IS IT WHERE WAS I? JUST TAKE US TO EASTERN AIR LINES!"

As impossible as it sounds, it was six o'clock and we were still checking into Eastern Air Lines. I couldn't even remember where we were going.

Of course this doesn't happen to me every time I fly. I'm the first one to admit that these were unusual circumstances. Everything went wrong. But take a more normal situation. I've flown many times when everything went just right. This is no great shakes either. Flying at its best is not the most comforting experience.

I keep seeing these ads in the travel section of the newspapers:

GETTING THERE IS HALF THE FUN

They're right. Just look at the fun. As soon as you enter the plane—all over the place, big red and white signs, "EMERGENCY EXIT." That's laughs.

Then you strap yourself down in your seat and a sign lights up over your head that says, "No Smoking." Inside the plane you shouldn't light a cigarette. Outside on the wings the engines are belching blue flames. This is very reassuring.

Since you can't smoke until you're in the air, there's really not much to do but sit back and relax. They've got a pocket in front of every seat that's stuffed with all sorts of goodies. There's a pamphlet called, "How to Use the Emergency Oxygen Equipment." There's an illustrated card of instructions titled, "Operating the Escape Slide." Special tips on "Bracing Yourself When Ditching."

I've got my own particular favorite—"101 Ways to Inflate Your Life Preserver."

For a clincher, every seat comes equipped with a white paper sack printed with the words, "FOR MOTION SICKNESS." Before a public-relations man got hold of it, they called it a "vomit bag." All I've got to do is look at the bag and I start getting ill.

Just about this time the stewardesses take over. They've got a little act they cooked up in stewardess school. The Andrews Sisters they're not.

"Ladies and gentlemen, Federal regulations require that we demonstrate the use of the emergency oxygen equipment located in the compartment directly over your head.

"In case of a sudden drop in cabin pressure, individual oxygen masks will drop out of each compartment. Grasp the mask firmly, hold it over your mouth, and breathe normally."

Have you got that? Breathe normally. The airplane is losing cabin pressure, but don't worry about it. All the air is rushing out, but that shouldn't bother you. All you've got to do is sit there and breathe normally. It's very important, because, if you don't YOU'RE GONNA TURN BLUE!

How's that for fun? It's a barrel of monkeys. But they're not through yet.

"Ladies and gentlemen, because we will be flying over water, Federal regulations require that we demonstrate the correct use of your life preserver.

"In the event of a ditching operation, do not inflate your preserver until you have left the plane."

Gives you sort of a deep-down feeling of security, doesn't it? I've been reading airline advertisements for years. I've never seen one word about an oxygen mask or a life preserver.

The big advertising campaigns now involve the relative benefits of first-class travel and tourist travel. On one hand, they tell you that you're crazy if you don't enjoy the luxury of first-class flight. On the other hand, they tell you you're crazy if you don't enjoy the economy of tourist-class travel. First class announces a rate reduction. Then tourist class announces a rate reduction.

I'm not sure who's crazy, but don't forget this is all the same airline. They make it sound like the front and the back of the plane were owned by two different companies.

They've done so much conflicting promotion on both classes of travel that most people are hopelessly confused. As an expert who has flown millions of air miles, both first class and tourist, I think I can clear up some of this confusion. All you've got to remember is that you don't get something for nothing.

First-class travel is just what its name implies, the ultimate in passenger service. On a round-trip flight between New York and Paris the difference is about $300 but it's worth it.

First-class passengers eat gourmet food prepared by the finest chefs in all Europe. Back in the tourist section—dry cheese sandwiches.

The menu alone is worth the price. Pâté de foie gras, artichoke bottoms en brochette, asparagus à la Polonaise, clams casino, squabs in cream sauce, strawberries au kirsch.

That's a great meal—until the plane hits an air pocket. WHOOPS! You just blew $300.

When you ride first class, you're a gentleman all the way. In the first place, a seat is reserved for you. As soon as you step on the plane, a beautiful stewardess takes your coat and leads you to the captain's Lounge. Right way she starts serving the booze.

Free cocktails, free champagne, free wine, free after-dinner drinks. When you get where you're going, it takes you three days to dry out. If you happen to be a member of Alcoholics Anonymous, it's worth $300 just to test your willpower.

The tourist passengers? They're not even on the plane yet. They're still out in the terminal. When you fly tourist, they herd you into something that resembles a prisoner-of-war compound. Then they open the gates. It looks like a newsreel shot of Chinese refugees fighting their way into Hong Kong.

There's a door in the plane that separates the two different classes of travel. As soon as you get on board, they close the door so the tourist passengers shouldn't see the orgy that's going on up in front.

Now in the first-class compartment they have what is known as "two and two" seating. This simply means that there are two seats on each side of the aisle. It's a rather cold and impersonal arrangement.

But in the back everything is warm and friendly—with the cattle, with the basketball teams, with the nursery. Four hundred kids, all screaming and yelling. You're flying to get away from your own children, and the plane looks like open house at morning kindergarten. All the stewardesses are nurses. They don't read the flight manual. Every six months they take a refresher course in Dr. Spock.

The tourist section has three seats on each side of the aisle. It's a cozy kind of arrangement. There's something intimate about being wedged between an airsick sailor and a young mother changing the diapers on her baby.

These are some of the big differences between the two types of accommodations. On the other hand, there are certain pleasures that everyone shares. All the seats are reclining seats. For some odd reason there's always one seat that reclines just a little bit more than the others and it always belongs to the guy who's sitting directly in front of you.

Then, too, everybody gets to listen to the same public-address system. As far as I'm concerned, this is a rather dubious privilege, because I usually end up with a pilot who won't shut up. Ten years ago he got a phone call from a research organization that wanted to know which television program he was watching. From that minute on he considered himself a part of the entertainment industry. He'd rather give up flying than quit "show biz."

"Ladies and gentlemen, hi y'all.

"This is your captain, Zip Anderson. I wanna welcome you aboard Trans-Eastern's Flight 803. We've leveled off at 40,000 feet. Our ground speed is 680 miles an hour. The temperature outside the plane is 47 degrees below zero. The temperature on the surface skin of the plane is 114 degrees above zero. The temperature of the co-pilot is 98.6 degrees Fahrenheit."

I've got a briefcase full of work that must be polished off before we land. Captain Midnight has a captive audience. To top it off, they're showing a feature-length movie. Up on the screen Dick Powell and Ruby Keeler are singing, "Don't Give Up the Ship."

"The weather in St. Louis is clear and seasonably cool with the temperature in the low fifties."

Good old Zip. He seems to know everything. I wonder if he knows we're going to Seattle.

"If you look out of the left side of the plane, you'll see a magnificent view of the Grand Canyon."

On the last trip he had called the same view to our attention. Only then he had said it was the Great Salt Lake.

Strangely enough, people usually speak about the advantages of *flying* first class. No one ever talks about the advantages of *landing* first class. This is very important, because it's a big status symbol. When your relatives are waiting at the airport, it always looks good if you come off the front of the plane.

Sometimes the airline fouls up and everybody leaves by the same exit. This can be pretty discouraging, but you should remember there are other benefits. Since you're flying in the front of the plane, you can always reach your destination first. If the plane comes in backward, they refund your money.

Well, now. That's my feeling about the airlines. I've been on hundreds of flights, traveled a million miles, and speak with authority—a fact that was acknowledged back in 1961 by the citation from the National Aviation Club of Washington: (see below)

Aviation Critics Award 1961
—— PRESENTED TO ——
Mr. Alan King

In recognition of the blasphemy this solon of suburbia has leveled at his unaccustomed target of aviation,

And in knowledge that space age air travel will be delayed for generations because of his gloomy approach to an otherwise normal landing,

With gratitude for his noble effort toward making the complaints of other aviation critics tolerable by comparison,

And in deference to his recognized, if somewhat macabre talent as a foremost humorist of our times,

Therefore Let It Be Known

That Mr. King, by singular impudence and cunning skill combined with devious intent, has proved to be the individual who, in 1960,

Contributed the Least to Aviation

Given, unhesitatingly, this 10th day of March, 1961, while in annual banquet assembled.

The National Aviation Club
Washington

———————————————
S. J. Solomon, President

CHAPTER 12

INSUFFICIENT FUNDS

HAVE YOU NOTICED that more and more of the advertising in newspapers and magazines and on radio and TV is directed to women? Not just those things that have always been a part of the female realm like beauty and cooking and decorating and fashion. I'm talking about products that have been traditionally a man's prerogative.

I have friends in the advertising and marketing profession who tell me that the wife is the one who decides on the family car and the television set and where to take the vacation. She buys her husband's socks and underwear and suits and even selects the house they'll live in.

So, men, it has finally happened, and we've no one to blame but ourselves. For years we let them nickel-and-dime us to death. Today they own us lock, stock, and barrel.

I mean that literally. Women control 80 percent of the wealth of this country. I just read this in one of the big financial magazines. Eighty percent! What they don't mention, though, is that the other 20 percent is controlled by bachelors. You show me a married millionaire, and I'll show you a pauper.

A woman will tell you that one of the great things about marriage is that it's a partnership. Then she gets married and goes into business for herself. For example, did you ever notice that there were two kinds of money in marriage? *Your* money and *her* money?

With *her* money she buys all the essentials for running

the household. Cigarettes, candy bars, and philodendra. With *your* money she makes up a shopping list that looks like the Dead Sea Scrolls.

Now I don't want to be unfair. In all honesty, my wife seldom asks me for money. Nine times out of ten Jeanette will go directly to my wallet and take it. She's the last of the Jesse James gang.

This doesn't bother me too much, because I know that most wives do the same thing. Sometimes even my mother-in-law will sneak in during the night and go through my pockets. Last week she was too busy, so she sent a friend. It's sort of a compulsion with women. What I object to is that my wife doesn't just steal a buck or two. She takes everything.

Can you imagine what it's like to be in New York City and suddenly find yourself without a penny. It happened to me last week.

I had to leave my watch with the train conductor. Then I tried to buy a subway token with a note Jeanette left in my wallet saying, "Sweetie Pie: I owe you $11.37." It didn't work.

I ran frantically from one end of Grand Central Station to the other looking for a familiar face who might lend me some money. After that I tried introducing myself to about thirty complete strangers, hoping to borrow fifteen cents until I could get to the office. They all threatened to call a cop. Not one of them thought I even looked like Alan King.

In desperation I opened my tie, ripped the front of my shirt, combed my hair down over my eyes and lurched up to the most likely looking prospect.

"Pardon me, shir," I mumbled, "but could you shpare a poor bum fifteen cents for a shot of cheap booze?"

I got the fifteen cents, but as I was staggering away I heard the guy who gave it to me turn to his friend and whisper, "Did you know that was Alan King?"

"Yeah," said the friend. "When they go, they go fast."

Now I'm not saying that Jeanette is an out-and-out spendthrift. To the contrary, about once every six months she goes on an economy binge that would bankrupt the House of Rothschild.

"Alan, we've been spending much too much money, and I think we ought to stay home this weekend."

"You really don't mind?"

"Of course I don't mind. We don't have to be running all of the time. There's no reason why we can't spend a nice quiet evening at home with a few close friends."

That's her idea of saving money. "A few close friends" consists of twenty couples united by a common bond—hunger—and a brother-in-law who drinks twelve-year-old Scotch for medicinal purposes. He's an alcoholic.

These low-budget parties are very common out in the suburbs. All the people are living so far beyond their means that they can't afford gas to drive into the city. The guests are supposed to bring their own liquor—and they do. About half of them bring 98-cent wine with a French label and drink my $6.50 bourbon. The others bring bottles with three shots left in them—the same three slugs they've been carrying from party to party for a year. They won't buy a new bottle until the old one evaporates.

There are no elaborate preparations for these parties. In fact, there's an agreement among the wives that the hostess won't cook. To most people this would mean coffee and cake. To Jeanette it means a catered affair.

Believe me, when Jeanette decides to economize, it isn't to save money. It's usually a plot to show me what life is going to be like unless I raise her allowance. I begin to get an idea of what's coming when she meets me at the door wearing sneakers, elastic stockings with rubber-band garters below the knees, and a canvas smock that the painters left in the garage two years ago.

My only hope is to remain nonchalant.

"Hello, dear. Been shopping with your mother again, I see."

"No, Alan. I just decided that I'm a big girl now. I'm going to have to learn to live within my allowance even if its means we'll be embarrassed and humiliated in front of your close friends and important business contacts."

Of course these veiled threats don't get her anywhere. But it's only the beginning. For the rest of the week I eat leftover food without once seeing the originals. Last week I came to the dinner table, and there she sat, big as life, with a full head of gray hair. This was the showdown!

"JEANETTE, WHAT ARE YOU DOING? WHAT'S THIS BIT WITH THE GRAY HAIR?"

"Now control yourself, Alan. I've decided to let my hair go to its natural color."

"WHADDAYA MEAN NATURAL COLOR? IT WAS BLACK THIS MORNING!"

"I'm sorry, Alan, but on my allowance I can't afford touch-ups anymore."

"WELL, WEAR A WIG; YOU'VE GOT EIGHT OF THEM. THERE'S ENOUGH HAIR IN YOUR CLOSET TO STUFF A MATTRESS."

"I'm afraid, Alan, that you're just going to have to give me more money."

I don't know what she's going to do with more money. She never pays for a purchase with cash. She thinks that if she doesn't pay cash, it's for free. Last year she was voted "Woman of the Year" by the Diners' Club.

My wife can write checks faster than I can tear them out of the checkbook. I wouldn't say she writes many checks, but all the people I know get their canceled checks in the mail. At my house they're delivered once a month by three trucks from American Van Lines.

Jeanette was the one who introduced me to a joint checking account—that's another name for alimony for married men. Before I was married, I'd worry all month if I couldn't find a five-cent mistake in my checkbook. Last week Jeanette wrote forty-two checks and made $3,200 worth of errors. She not only added up the checks, she added in the day and the year. She not only added it in, but I paid it.

Are you one of those people who misses the championship fights they used to show on television? Well, you have an open invitation to come over to my house on the first of any month. That's the time I get the bank statement. It really comes on the twenty-fifth of the month, but my wife hides it on the outside chance that, between the twenty-fifth and the first, I'll reveal that I'm not really Alan King but the eldest son of the Aga Khan.

In the first place, I balance a bank statement like everyone else balances a bank statement. I start by putting the checks in numerical order—and that's when the indigestion begins.

Half the checks don't have any number at all. At least ten of them all have the same number, and the rest of the checks would make more sense if they were copied from the patent rights on a box of cornflakes. For example, Jeanette paid the last grocery bill on September 38.

This in itself is not so bad. There are more serious things, like finding a blank stub in the checkbook.

"Jeanette, what's this blank stub in the checkbook?"

"Where, Alan, honey?"

"Right here, Jeanette, dear. Between the eighty-six-dollar check to your hairdresser and the fourteen-cent check to the Good Humor man."

"I'm very tired, Alan. I think I'm going to bed."

"It's three o'clock in the afternoon. How much was the check for?"

"I just remembered."

"Good. Whisper in my ear."

"It was for either $17.98 or $89.71."

"But you haven't got $89.71 in your checking account. It's gonna bounce."

"Alan, can you lend me $89.71 until next Wednesday?"

That's what my wife calls fighting fire with heartburn. I can't win. When we got married I was making $35 a week. It was good enough for her then. I had to go out and borrow money so she could go on a honeymoon. I couldn't afford to go along with her.

Things have changed since then. The government has been trying to get my wife down to Washington for ten years now. She's one of the few people in the country who understands deficit spending. The bank in our neighborhood has three different windows. One is marked "paying," one is marked "receiving," and one is marked "Jeanette King."

And that's some bank we deal with. It's got more branches than Queen Elizabeth's family tree.

I remember when banks were dignified, conservative institutions. You deposited money for safekeeping and convenience and withdrew your money when you needed it. For this privilege you were charged a small fee and the bank made a small profit. If you had substantial references, an unimpeachable character, an adequate income, three cosigners, and collateral to cover, there was a fair chance that you could negotiate a loan.

Today's bank is a cross between the Paris Flea Market and the pari-mutuel windows at Santa Anita. Believe me, I speak from experience. Between my wife, my two sons, and me, we have nine checking accounts and sixty-one savings accounts. Jeanette found out that every time she opened a new account for more than five dollars, the bank gave her a ball-point pen, a transistor radio, a nonstick fry pan, and a forty-eight-cup coffeepot. If you open an account on a Thursday night, you can get ten shirts ironed free of charge.

In my neighborhood alone two discount stores and a Chinese laundry closed because they couldn't stand the competition.

Now that might be an exaggeration, but it's not a big one. So help me, one of the biggest banks in the city has an ice carnival in its window every winter, and once a year it has a tulip exhibit with so many bulbs that Holland has been able to drop its plans for a national lottery.

Modern banking is getting too confusing. It wasn't long ago that my average monthly balance was just under four dollars. If Jeanette wrote a check for ten dollars, that didn't mean the check would bounce. The bank would honor it and hold it and I'd get a call from one of the officers who'd ask me to come in and cover my last withdrawal.

Today my average balance is over $1,000 and I wouldn't know a vice-president from the office boy—which is a poor comparison because the office boy *is* a vice-president.

My bank is about as personal as a crack in the sidewalk. If I'm one dollar overdrawn, nobody calls me. There's no time for that anymore. They're all acting in TV commercials. Instead, they've got an electronic brain that records the whole transaction and sends out a warrant for my arrest.

Actually, it isn't a warrant. It's one of those electronic punch cards with holes all over and it reads:

YO A COUN IS O ERDR N.
WE ARE R URNING UR C E K
AND CHAR ING YOU $ .99.

I can't read it. I don't have to. What's frightening is I'm
beginning to understand it.

Every other building in New York is owned by a bank,
but they can't afford to send me a letter on a whole piece
of paper. The only thing that makes sense is a notice in
the corner that says, "Do not fold, staple, spindle, or mu-
tilate this card." That I can read.

In the meantime, the person I gave the check to originally gets it back stamped on both sides in blood-red
letters, "INSUFFICIENT FUNDS." This person, of
course, is never my family doctor, the butcher, or my
brother-in-law. It's the membership chairman of the golf
club that's taken five years to get around to my applica-
tion.

So figure it out. If I use more of my own money than
I've got on deposit, the whole roof falls in. If I want to use
somebody else's money, the bank can't give it away fast
enough. I took out a loan on a car for Jeanette, and I
didn't even sign a paper. I had one of the kids run down
to the bank to pick it up. He came back with the money,
a payment book, and enough Green Stamps for a two-
week vacation in Miami.

Khrushchev could walk in tomorrow and get a home-
improvement loan on the Kremlin.

In fact, he doesn't even have to come to the bank. Bank
by mail is the thing to do these days. Better yet, you can
"Bank by phone." Or you can even "Bank by car." Now
they have drive-in banks. You drive your car right up to
the teller's window and he fills up your trunk.

This doesn't mean that you don't have to pay the money
back eventually. That's what the payment book is for. You
open it up and the first thing you find is "Installment
Ticket 1." That sort of gives you the idea that the next
page is "Installment Ticket 2." Well, you're wrong.

Page two is a pea-green insert with an invitation from
the bank to come in and borrow more money.

Now that they've got your first payment, they don't

know what to do with it. It's burning a hole in their pockets. For a modest 5½ percent you can have it all back plus a new payment book with baby-blue inserts.

The last page of the payment book is still another plea to come down and pick up another bundle of cash—only this one you can't afford to ignore. Whatever you bought with the money in the first place is about to fall apart.

Friday morning I paid the final installment on the car. Friday afternoon Jeanette called me to say that the motor fell out in the driveway. After thirty-six installments, my canceled checks have greater resale value than the whole car with a full tank of gasoline.

Do you think it's a coincidence? Not on your life. The day I paid off the television set, the picture disappeared and all I got was snow—on the outside of the set.

I remember when people used to go to banks because they were the only place they could leave their money with confidence. Today they can go into a bank just because they're lonely.

That's the truth. Watch the TV commercials any night of the week. I'm still trying to figure out who pays for all this bank advertising. Somewhere between the teller's cage and the bank vaults, my money must make an awfully long detour.

At any rate, the different TV commercials all try to convince you that the bank that's advertising is the friendliest bank in the city. Well, friends I've already got. I'd rather have more sarcasm and pay less interest.

Tell your friendly bank that you can't make the payment on your auto loan. They'll laugh jovially. They'll shake your hand. They'll pat you on the back. They'll take away your car. If all these banks are as friendly as they say they are, how come they chain all the fountain pens to the desk?

Go into the bank someday and meet some of your friends. You no sooner walk in the door and you get the once-over from a guy in uniform with two six-shooters strapped to his waist. This is the bank guard. Every time he looks my way I feel like I have the combination to the safe tattooed on my forehead. Any minute now. Pow! A piece of lead right between the eyes.

The next friendly person you encounter is the bank teller. He's the guy who's always in the next window. A bank may have twenty tellers' cages, but it has only one teller. All of the cages but one have little signs saying "Next Window, Please." You can spot him quickly if you look for a line that goes out the door and around the block.

The line moves rather slowly, because the teller is always a cautious and meticulous man. He has to be very careful that he doesn't run out of saliva. Nothing could be worse than counting money with a dry thumb. A good teller is a moist teller. For this he goes through a two-year executive training program.

I can shake $500 out of my son's piggy bank in less time than it takes to cash a check at my own bank. In fact, most of the time I find it easier just to borrow money from my friendly kids. They get all they want from their friendly mother who steals all she wants from her friendly husband.

Next week I'm going to start my own advertising campaign. We're a very friendly family. Do you need money? Why don't you come in and see us?

CHAPTER 13

WELCOME HOME

MODERN MAN IS expected to be a good provider for his family, a faithful and virile husband, a helpmate, a loving father, an asset to his community, a paragon of virtue, a pillar of strength, a fountain of compassion. And all the time he's got to conform to the system, act by the rules, and live by the numbers.

Is it any wonder that he's neurotic? Is it any wonder that he has an ulcer and sucks on tranquilizers like they were Sen-Sen? This poor guy gets up at 7 A.M., argues with his wife, battles his kids, swallows breakfast in one big lump, fights traffic into the city, gets trampled in the public conveyances, breathes polluted air, and risks life and limb just to cross the street.

As soon as he gets to work, he's hounded by the bank, threatened by his creditors, and works under constant tensions, pressures, and insecurities while he's being undercut by his competitors, abused by his boss, and stabbed in the back by his associates.

Five o'clock he gets back into the car, fights the bumper-to-bumper traffic all over again, staggers up to his house and throws himself across the threshold into the waiting arms of his loving wife who speaks the first kind words he's heard in ten hours:

"I'M GOING TO HAVE A NERVOUS BREAK-DOWN!"

Get that, will you? He's just returned from the Seven Years' War and the Spanish Inquisition. His wife didn't get out of bed until noon. The biggest decision she had to make all day was whether or not to meld a joker canasta—but *she's* going to have a nervous breakdown.

And every night they hit you with something just a little bit different. This helps to break up the monotony. Marriage should never become routine.

"Don't take off your coat. We're going out to dinner. If I have to spend one more minute in this lousy house I'll go stark, raving mad."

Mind you, now, this is the same cookie who, ten years ago, was pleading for a little place we could call our own. That's all she wanted. "Alan, buy us a house in the country and I promise that I'll never ask for another thing as long as I live."

When Jeanette promises never to ask for another thing, it's like Hitler saying, "All I want is Czechoslovakia."

Do you know why she wants to go out for dinner? She just got home from her voodoo class. Dinner isn't ready. In fact, it isn't even started, but she won't admit it. She's got to perform the whole last act from *Camille* followed by a chorus of the largo from "Death and Transfiguration." She takes all the parts.

Just once maybe I'll come home from work and I'll hear, "Darling, I've had a wonderful day," or maybe, "Honey, I feel just great." Never! It has something to do with female hormones. The minute I pull the car into the garage she don't feel so good. You can imagine how much sympathy I'm going to get.

"To tell you the truth, Jeanette, I don't feel so good either."

"Alan, I said it first."

That's right. She did say it first. This is very important, because they've all got to have the first word, and they've all got to have the last word. If you get a headache, you don't say, "I have a headache." You have to wait and see if she has a headache.

She says, "I have a headache." Now she's had the first word. Immediately she starts to feel better.

At this point it's perfectly okay for you to say, "I have a headache, too."

She says, "I said it first." That's the last word.

It's like a game. The winner goes into the finals at Forest Lawn Cemetery.

It's all great fun, of course, and right away I can feel the digestive juices going to work on the raw lining of my empty stomach. Mostly, my nerves are as taut as piano strings after a day in the competitive jungle of big business. In eighteen years of marriage Jeanette has learned to recognize the signs.

"Honey, you're so tense and jumpy."

"Tough day."

"I'll bet it was. Come sit over here on the sofa and I'll rub your forehead."

"Good idea. Hmmmm. Ahhhh."

"Like it?"

"Great!"

"We got a notice from the bank that we're overdrawn. The dog bit a policeman. They can't fix the refrigerator, so we'll have to get a new one. Alan, for heaven's sake, relax."

"Tough day."

"I know, dear. The dentist says that Andy needs orthodontia. The garage called and said the car needs a ring job, whatever that is. There's a letter on your dresser from the Internal Revenue Service. Are you ready to eat?"

Am I ready to eat? I'm ready to go back to the office. That competitive jungle is starting to look like the Garden of Eden.

"Yes, I'm ready to eat."

"Fine. What would you like for dinner?"

Right away a wave of relief sweeps over me. For a while I was afraid she might have prepared dinner without consulting me.

"How about a teaspoon of hot consommé? I haven't eaten in sixteen hours. I don't wanna shock my stomach."

Some husbands come home and their wives have dinner waiting for them. They don't have a chance to unwind and relax. Jeanette is very considerate that way. Some-

135

times she'll just eliminate dinner and we'll go right into breakfast.

Now any man who works all day in a white shirt and a tie and a vest and a suit coat knows what a pleasure it is to come home and slip into something more comfortable. I've got a pair of old corduroy pants, a sweat shirt, and bunny slippers that I call my "relaxing outfit." My wife refers to it as my "slob suit," which is not a term of endearment. She hates it. She went to the same movie three times to watch Marlon Brando walk around in torn underwear, but there's a moth hole in my sweat shirt. That she finds repulsive.

"What did you do with my relaxing outfit?"

"I put it where it belongs—in the garbage."

"Are you gonna leave my clothes alone? I like that outfit."

"You can't walk around the house like that. I think my friend Millie is coming over."

"I can't wait. I'm gonna run in and put on my tuxedo."

"I read in a movie magazine that Richard Burton walks around his house wearing a velvet smoking jacket."

"All right. When you start looking like Elizabeth Taylor, I'll start dressing like Richard Burton."

At this point in the evening festivities I usually pull a pillow off the bed, carry it into the den, and stretch out on the couch. It never fails. The minute I put my head back it's like she has built-in radar. Her dulcet voice comes floating in from the kitchen.

"ALAN! DON'T GET TOO COMFORTABLE. DINNER WILL BE READY IN FIVE MINUTES."

That's nice. If I was cutting the grass, dinner would be ready in two hours. Besides, I'm not ready for dinner. I need to get emotionally prepared first, because now I've got to sit down at the table with my two charming sons. All day long I'm getting cut up into little pieces by a bunch of amateurs. It's a real pleasure to come home and get worked over by a couple of professionals.

"Andy, take your finger out of your nose."

"But there's something . . ."

"WE'RE EATING DINNER. I DON'T WANNA DISCUSS THE DETAILS."

Now I've got to contend with Jeanette. "Alan, you don't have to yell at the children."

I don't have to breathe, either, but I yell and I breathe because it's the only way I can survive. I yell at the kids, because I haven't got the guts to yell at my wife. This is what the psychiatrists call "transference." Sometimes I take a swipe at the dog for good measure.

"AND WHO LEFT THE TELEVISION SET ON?"

"Bobby did it, Daddy. Bobby did it." That's Andy, the family stoolpigeon. He's not above stretching the truth just to see his brother get clobbered.

"Gee, Dad, I'm listening to Yogi Bear."

"That's why I bought an $800 color-television set for the den. So we can all sit in the dining room and listen to Yogi Bear. TURN IT OFF!"

Let me tell you a secret. It's not my idea that we all eat together. Jeanette insists that the children should get a chance to chat leisurely while they're breaking bread with their father. She's got a good point there, and in theory it's fine. I really believe that talking with my kids can be an enlightening and rewarding experience. Looking at them is a different story. That can make you a little sick.

If they gave grades in school for being dirty, my two sons could flunk all their other subjects and still get scholarships to Harvard.

When they come to the dinner table, the older one usually looks like he slid into third base on his mouth. The younger one is filthy from head to toe. He's got creases in his neck where the Spanish moss is starting to grow.

"Andy, get into the bathroom and wash your face."

Two minutes later he's back. "How's that, Dad?"

"That's fine. Now go back into the bathroom and dry your face."

"Holy cow. Why don'tcha make up your mind?" It's wonderful to have the respect of your children.

Next it's Bobby's turn. I gotta send 'em in separately, so they don't clog the sink. It's the same routine all over again, only this kid is truly a genius. I still haven't figured out how he washes his face without getting his hands wet.

Now if you're one of those people who has trouble losing weight, forget about those drugs, exercises, and fad diets. Come over to my house and have dinner with my kids. It's like a three-round preliminary to the main event. The main event, of course, comes later. That's when we try to get them to bed.

ROUND ONE: *Can I have some mustard, Dad?* You don't put mustard on spaghetti. *I want mustard.* You can't have mustard. It doesn't taste good on spaghetti. *It tastes good to me.* Well, it isn't good for you. *Why?* Because when you put mustard on spaghetti, your father gives you a smack. That's why it isn't good for you.

ROUND TWO: *What's that?* That's broccoli. It tastes very good. *I don't like it.* Whaddaya mean, you don't like it? You never tasted it before. *I can tell. I don't like it.* Taste it, and if you don't like it, you won't have to eat it. *No!* Taste it or you won't have any dessert. *No!* Taste it or you're gonna get a smack. *I'll throw up.* Good. When you finish, come back to the table and eat the broccoli.

ROUND THREE: *Dad, Andy is kicking me under the table.* Andy, stop kicking your brother under the table. *Okay.* Thank you. *You're welcome.* Now stop kicking your father under the table. *You drank Coke out of my glass.* I did? I'm sorry. Here, I'll pour you some more. *I want a clean glass.* There's nothing wrong with that glass. *You had your mouth on it.* I'M YOUR FATHER! *You got germs.* SO DO YOUR DIRTY FINGERNAILS, BUT IT

138

DOESN'T STOP YOU FROM BITING THEM. *What's for dessert?* BROCCOLI! *Mom, look at Dad. He's got his elbows on the table again.* SO HELP ME, YOU'RE BOTH GONNA GET A SHOT . . .

Do you think I get any help from my wife? Not on your life. All through dinner she sits there with that "now-you-know-what-I-go-through-all-day" smile on her face. There's only one thing that gives me the courage to get through dinner. I keep thinking that as soon as it's over I'm going to get back to the couch.

After a good meal I could lie down on that couch and be asleep in ten seconds if they'd only let me alone. But there's something peculiar about women. They just can't stand to see you lying on the couch. The kids jump on the couch, they drip ice cream on it, the dog sprawls all over it, but when I lie down, she gives me a whole list of instructions:

"Don't put your head back because you'll get grease from your hair on the arm . . .

"Don't put your feet up because you'll dirty the cushions . . .

"Relax."

I shouldn't put my head down. I shouldn't put my feet up. I should relax. Doesn't everyone relax with his head on the floor, his fanny on the couch, and his feet hanging out the window? I happen to like this position, but it doesn't mean that now I'm going to take a nap. There's no rest for the weary, because right away in the other part of the house my wife is using the latest psychological approach to putting the children to bed.

"CAN'T STAND IT ANYMORE! YOU'RE KILLING ME! GET TO SLEEP THIS MINUTE! IF YOU DON'T GO TO BED, I'M SENDING YOUR FATHER UP."

Sure enough, a minute later Jeanette comes running into the den.

"Alan, put them to sleep."

139

"I wish you would fight with me to go to sleep. I've been trying to shut my eyes for three hours."

(If there are any kids who happen to be reading this book, I'd like to interject a few words of advice here. Boys and girls, you should always go to sleep when your parents tell you. You need your sleep now, because you're gonna grow up and you're gonna have kids of your own and then there's no sleeping.)

And, boy, can they stall! They have one slogan: Five minutes more. And when nothing else works, the little angels suddenly remember that they didn't say their prayers. Well, after all, you've got to let them say their prayers. Then they start.

"Bless Mommy. Bless Daddy, Grandpa Bernie, Grandma Minnie, Grandpa Izzie, Grandma Bella. Bless Huckleberry Hound, Yogi Bear, Mighty Mouse, Rocky the Flying Squirrel . . ."

"ROCKY THE FLYING SQUIRREL? GO TO SLEEP."

"Oh, please, Daddy. Won't you tell us a story? One little story?"

It's amazing. All day long these miserable creatures are driving you crazy. You can't wait until they go to bed so maybe you can have at least one hour of peace and tranquillity. But then it happens. They're all washed up, tucked under the covers, their innocent little faces framed against their pillows, and all of a sudden your heart goes out to them. If I could keep them in bed twenty-four hours a day, there wouldn't be any problems.

"All right. Just one. Don't forget, just one and that's it."

"Could you tell us the story about the three bears?"

These kids have minds like steel traps. They've got a copy of *Fanny Hill* hidden in their closet, so when they ask for "The Three Bears," already I'm a little suspicious.

"Okay. Once there were three bears."

"No, Daddy. *Once upon a time* there were three bears."

"All right. Once upon a time there were three bears. There was the momma bear, the poppa bear, and the baby bear. Right?"

"Right."

"One day they went for a walk in the park."

"No, Daddy. They went for a walk in the forest."

140

"These three bears went for a walk in the forest. Then they came home and found Little Red Riding Hood . . . What's so funny?"

"No, Daddy. They found Goldilocks. But first the poppa bear said, 'Who's been eating my porridge?' Then the momma bear said . . ."

"This time you're wrong. That's the old version. This is the new version. Momma Bear got into her bed. Poppa Bear got into his bed, and he said to the little baby bear, 'If you don't stop stalling and go to sleep, you're gonna get a rap in the mouth.' GET TO SLEEP!"

Now I come back into the den and, believe it or not, somebody is sleeping on *my* couch—and it isn't Goldilocks.

"Come on, Jeanette. I'm tired. Why don't you let me lie down?"

"If you're so tired, why don't you put on your pajamas and go to bed?"

I know that sounds like a legitimate question, but it never works out that way. The minute I put on my pajamas, I'm wide-awake. There's no sleeping, because as soon as I crawl into bed, my wife turns the "Late Show" on full blast. Did you ever try to sleep through the marines landing on Iwo Jima? Of course I doze off eventually, and when I do it's a signal to Jeanette that it's time for her to take a shower.

"It's three in the morning. Whaddaya taking a shower? I'm trying to sleep."

"I want to be clean," she says.

"Can't you be clean quietly? Why don't you get some of those cleaning pads—nice and quiet?"

An hour later she's still in the shower. The steam is pouring out of the bathroom door, the wallpaper is starting to peel, and the bedroom looks like a foggy night in London town. I not only can't sleep, I'm having trouble breathing.

"Will you come on already?"

"Alan, get me a towel."

"I'm in bed, remember? Dry yourself with your nylons. That's the only thing I ever find hanging in the bathroom anyway."

After the shower she walks in with the cream, the

curlers, and the chin strap. Now I'm too frightened to fall asleep, but, just in case I do, Jeanette takes care of that, too. When she goes to bed, her mind is still functioning. By this time I'm in a coma, but she wants to talk.

"Alan?" she says, giving me the elbow in the ribs. It's like being harpooned.

"What is it, Jeanette?"

"Want to take me out to dinner tomorrow night?"

"I'll take you out to dinner. I'll take you dancing. Will you let me sleep?"

"Should I wear the black or the green dress?"

"Wear a bathing suit. I'll take you for seafood. Will you let me sleep?"

"But, Alan, I never get a chance to talk to you."

"YOU NEVER GET A CHANCE TO TALK TO ME! THEN THERE'S ANOTHER BROAD IN THIS HOUSE WITH A VERY BIG MOUTH."

This, of course, insults her and she refuses to say another word. I wish I would have thought of it five hours ago, because, if I'm lucky, I'll get only two hours' sleep before the alarm clock goes off. "Lucky" is my middle name, because now the parade starts. First the little one gets up and he climbs right into the bed.

"What can I do for you?"

"I'm scared."

"Whaddaya scared of?"

"The poppa bear gave the baby bear a rap in the mouth."

Two minutes later the big one knows that the little one's in our bed, so he gets up and joins the group.

"Welcome aboard."

Then the rotten dog, he don't want to be left alone. He comes in and joins, and I've got a mob scene lying there. Mind you, all I wanted was a little sleep. Is that too much to ask for? My wife's got her cold feet on top of mine. The little one's got his finger in my ear like a bowling ball, the big one has his foot in my mouth, and the dog is jumping on my head.

I've heard of togetherness, but this is ridiculous.

. . . .

Well, there you have it. That's how my day begins, ends, and just a few of the things in between.

Right now it's 6 A.M. in the King household, and everyone is sound asleep except me. It's so nice and peaceful out here in the garage, and I don't have to be afraid that my typing will wake anyone up. Did I say "afraid"? I meant "terrified."

Through a window I can see the first golden rays of the sun creeping over the horizon. The sound of the crickets is being replaced by the frantic morning chatter of the birds in search of food for their hungry young. And I can't think of a better way to end a book than to sort of fade out against a magnificent sunrise sparkling on the crystalline blue waters of Long Island Sound. The yellow roses against the verdant evergreens. Dew shimmering on grass rippled by the gentle eastern breeze. It's times like these that make it all seem worthwhile.

There's not a soul on the sidewalks. Not a car on the streets except the police car patrolling the beat with two policemen in it, and I find them reassuring. Champions of the law. Defenders of our fundamental right to life, liberty, and the pursuit of happiness.

—Top of the morning to you, officers. Wonderful day, isn't it?

—I beg your pardon, officer?

—I always sit in my garage in my pajamas and watch the sunrise. Doesn't everybody sit in his garage in his pajamas and watch the sunrise?

—Whaddaya mean, indecent exposure? I'm wearing pajamas. This is my own damn garage.

—If I was planning to commit suicide, I wouldn't sit with the garage door open and say "good morning" to the first stupid bulls who drove by.

—Look, officer. I'm Alan King, the comedian. You know, television, nightclubs, the theater. I've been living here for ten years.

—Of course I don't have my driver's license. I left it in my other pajamas.

—Don't ring the doorbell. You'll wake everybody up.

143

—I SAID DON'T RING THE . . . ! You did it, didn't you?
—You did.

oh, my God, here we go again
help
i'm a prisoner in a Chinese bakery